Gospel Connections for Teens

Gospel Connections for Teens

Reflections for Sunday Mass, Cycle C

Corey Brost, CSV

saint mary's press

The publishing team included Brian Singer-Towns, development editor; Lorraine Kilmartin, reviewer; prepress and manufacturing coordinated by the prepublication and production services departments of Saint Mary's Press.

Printed in the United States of America

3441

ISBN 978-0-88489-641-8

Library of Congress Cataloging-in-Publication Data
Brost, Corey.
Gospel connections for teens : reflections for Sunday mass / Corey Brost.
   v. cm.
Contents: — [2] Cycle C.
ISBN 978-0-88489-641-8 (v. 2 : pbk.)
   1. Bible. N.T. Gospels—Meditations—Juvenile literature. 2. Church year meditations—Juvenile literature. I. Title.
BS2555.54.B76 2006
242'.63—dc22

2005000795

I dedicate this book to my brother and sister Viatorians, especially those who have stood by me for many years. Your faith, patience, support, challenge, and humor have shown me the face of God. You have made me a more faithful disciple and have helped me find life to the fullest (see John 10:10). And for that, I can't thank you enough.

This book was a joint effort. Four teens worked diligently as an editing team to help me refine each reflection. Their input was invaluable. So thanks to Rosanne Cruz, John Leahy, Kate Schwarz, and Celine Fitzgerald. Your willingness to grow closer to Christ has inspired me.

Contents

Introduction

I wrote this book because I never had one like it when I was a teen. I struggled each Sunday to connect the Gospel to my teen ups and downs. I hope this book helps you do just that.

First, a brief explanation. In the Church liturgical year, the Sunday Gospel readings follow a three-year cycle. This book covers the third year of that cycle, called cycle C. In cycle C most of the Gospel readings are taken from the Gospel of Luke.

Here's how you use this book, then. Look at the chart that follows this introduction. Look up the date of the coming Sunday in the chart, and you will find the correct reflection. Commit to spending twenty minutes each week reflecting on the Gospel before you go to Mass. Use the book's reflection process or create your own. Then go to Mass on Sunday and compare your reflection to the homily. You might even want to get a few friends together over coffee or snacks during the week to compare thoughts on the readings.

Because of space limitations, I've edited a few lines out of some of the Gospel passages. The Scripture citations at the top of the page indicate the complete Gospel passage for that Sunday. If I've shortened the passage, you will see a second citation immediately following the passage, indicating the exact verses I used.

All but a few of the names in the reflections are made up, though all the people I mention are real people I've come across in life and ministry.

Reflection Chart

Sunday Gospel Reflection	Page No.	2015–2016	2018–2019	2021–2022
1st Sunday of Advent	14	Nov. 29	Dec. 2	Nov. 28
2nd Sunday of Advent	16	Dec. 6	Dec. 9	Dec. 5
3rd Sunday of Advent	18	Dec. 13	Dec. 16	Dec. 12
4th Sunday of Advent	20	Dec. 20	Dec. 23	Dec. 19
Christmas Day	22	Dec. 25	Dec. 25	Dec. 25
Holy Family	24	Dec. 27	Dec. 30	Dec. 26
Mary, Mother of God	26	Jan. 1	Jan. 1	Jan. 1
Epiphany Sunday	28	Jan. 3	Jan. 6	Jan. 2
Baptism of the Lord	30	Jan. 10	Jan. 13	Jan. 9
2nd Sunday in Ordinary Time	32	Jan. 17	Jan. 20	Jan. 16
3rd Sunday in Ordinary Time	34	Jan. 24	Jan. 27	Jan. 23
4th Sunday in Ordinary Time	36	Jan. 31	Feb. 3	Jan. 30
5th Sunday in Ordinary Time	38	Feb. 7	Feb. 10	Feb. 6
6th Sunday in Ordinary Time	40		Feb. 17	Feb. 13
7th Sunday in Ordinary Time	42		Feb. 24	Feb. 20
8th Sunday in Ordinary Time	44		Mar. 3	Feb. 27
1st Sunday of Lent	46	Feb. 14	Mar. 10	Mar. 6
2nd Sunday of Lent	48	Feb. 21	Mar. 17	Mar. 13
3rd Sunday of Lent	50	Feb. 28	Mar. 24	Mar. 20
4th Sunday of Lent	52	Mar. 6	Mar. 31	Mar. 27
5th Sunday of Lent	54	Mar. 13	April 7	April 3
Palm Sunday (The Passion)	56	Mar. 20	April 14	April 10
Easter Sunday	58	Mar. 27	April 21	April 17
2nd Sunday of Easter	60	April 3	April 28	April 24
3rd Sunday of Easter	62	April 10	May 5	May 1
4th Sunday of Easter	64	April 17	May 12	May 8
5th Sunday of Easter	66	April 24	May 19	May 15
6th Sunday of Easter	68	May 1	May 26	May 22
7th Sunday of Easter	70	May 8	June 2	May 29

Reflections on the
Sunday Gospel Readings

Freedom Is Coming

Take :05 Examine

How did I live out last week's Gospel message? What was tough? What was rewarding?

Take :05 Read

Jesus said to his disciples: "There will be signs in the sun, the moon, and the stars, and on earth nations will be in dismay, perplexed by the roaring of the sea and the waves. People will die of fright in anticipation of what is coming upon the world, for the powers of the heavens will be shaken. And then they will see the Son of Man coming in a cloud with power and great glory. But when these signs begin to happen, stand erect and raise your heads because your redemption is at hand.

"Beware that your hearts do not become drowsy from carousing and drunkenness and the anxieties of daily life, and that day catch you by surprise like a trap. For that day will assault everyone who lives on the face of the earth. Be vigilant at all times and pray that you have the strength to escape the tribulations that are imminent and to stand before the Son of Man."

I remember my first day of high school. I was scared. We had just moved into town and I didn't know anyone in the freshman class. I was scared the seniors might beat me up. I was scared of not making friends. I was scared of looking foolish.

Many teens struggle with fear today. I know teens that are afraid of failing tests and teens that are afraid of losing friends. I know teens that are afraid of gangs and violence. Fear is pretty normal, so don't feel ashamed if you feel it.

Just think about Luke's Gospel. Early Christians knew fear. Many were persecuted. Many thought the world might end any day. So Luke wanted them to remember Jesus' words when he wrote his Gospel.

When you feel fear "stand erect and raise your heads because your redemption is at hand." Where can you get this courage? Luke tells us to pray and be vigilant, which means we must think carefully about a Christian response before important decisions.

So this Advent, remember Luke's confidence. He knew that disciplined Christians could stand proudly, face their fears, and not be controlled by their fears. God might not remove that which scares us, but God gives us courage to live with integrity. The courage to live without surrendering to the "anxieties of daily life," whether those anxieties come from tests, family, gangs, or friends.

Jesus *is* coming again this holiday season to free you from the fears that can control you. Spend extra time in prayer. Be more vigilant about the way you follow Jesus in your daily life. Do these things, and you'll know God is with you.

Take :10 Reflect

If a word or phrase from the Gospel grabs your heart, sit quietly for several minutes, repeating it to yourself and asking God to show you how it applies to your life. Or, reflect and possibly journal on the following questions:

• What worries do I most need Jesus to free me from? What can I do this Advent to let Jesus come closer to me?

Get Out of That Mainstream!

Take :05 Examine

How did I live out last week's Gospel message? What was tough? What was rewarding?

Take :05 Read

In the fifteenth year of the reign of Tiberius Caesar, when Pontius Pilate was governor of Judea, and Herod was tetrarch of Galilee, and his brother Philip tetrarch of the region of Ituraea and Trachonitis, and Lysanias was tetrarch of Abilene, during the high priesthood of Annas and Caiaphas, the word of God came to John the son of Zechariah in the desert. John went throughout the whole region of the Jordan, proclaiming a baptism of repentance for the forgiveness of sins, as it is written in the book of the words of the prophet Isaiah:

A voice of one crying out in the desert:
"Prepare the way of the Lord,
   make straight his paths.
Every valley shall be filled
   and every mountain and hill shall be made low.
The winding roads shall be made straight,
   and the rough ways made smooth,
and all flesh shall see the salvation of God."

I remember a senior in high school telling me one day that everyone at school knows she doesn't drink, do drugs, or have sex. I can't remember our exact conversation, but I do remember her confidence in the way she chose to live. She was a popular student too, but she was "out of the mainstream," according to some.

In many ways, she was like John the Baptist, "a voice . . . crying out in the desert." John, like many religious leaders through history, removed himself from society's mainstream to promote a different message—a message that wasn't popular but was good for the people. "Change your lives," he was calling out, "You're on the wrong paths, even though it doesn't seem like it and even though those paths are leading you away from God."

Today, just like in John's time, there are a lot of paths out there. And many paths that are promoted for teens just lead teens away from God. Drug and alcohol use. Sex before marriage. Gang lifestyle. Those are a few paths some people promote or accept. Each one can lead to what seems like good things at first. But eventually, statistics show, these paths lead to dead ends like broken relationships, single teen parenthood, addiction, violence, or jail.

God wants much more for you. So God has sent you people like John the Baptist. People that can live happy and healthy lives while changing the world. People that point to paths that will lead you to be all God knows you can be, if you watch or listen to them. My friend the senior in high school was such a voice. I don't know how many people she influenced. But I do know she was proud of her values. They helped her build strong self-esteem.

Can you be a voice in the wilderness this Advent by showing your peers the path to God? If not, can you listen closely this Advent for the voices pointing out new paths for you?

Take :10 Reflect

If a word or phrase from the Gospel grabs your heart, sit quietly for several minutes, repeating it to yourself and asking God to show you how it applies to your life. Or, reflect and possibly journal on the following questions:

- Is your life on a path you'd like to change? What people do you admire for following the Christian path?

What's On Your Christmas List?

Take :05 Examine

How did I live out last week's Gospel message? What was tough? What was rewarding?

Take :05 Read

The crowds asked John the Baptist, "What should we do?" He said to them in reply, "Whoever has two cloaks should share with the person who has none. And whoever has food should do likewise." Even tax collectors came to be baptized and they said to him, "Teacher, what should we do?" He answered them, "Stop collecting more than what is prescribed." Soldiers also asked him, "And what is it that we should do?" He told them, "Do not practice extortion, do not falsely accuse anyone, and be satisfied with your wages."

Now the people were filled with expectation, and all were asking in their hearts whether John might be the Christ. John answered them all, saying, "I am baptizing you with water, but one mightier than I is coming. I am not worthy to loosen the thongs of his sandals. He will baptize you with the Holy Spirit and fire. His winnowing fan is in his hand to clear his threshing floor and to gather the wheat into his barn, but the chaff he will burn with unquenchable fire." Exhorting them in many other ways, he preached good news to the people.

I remember Christmastime as a kid and young adult. I spent a lot of time worrying about whether I'd get all the stuff I'd hoped for.

My attitude started changing as I grew closer to Jesus. One Christmas some friends took me someplace that changed my Christmas hopes completely—a soup kitchen.

These friends visited a soup kitchen each Christmas Day. While other volunteers served food, my friends sang carols. They sang about the Good News while hungry men, women, and children—many who were also homeless—lined up for their holiday meal. During that first Christmas visit, I wondered how long it had been since anyone had given some of those hungry folks good news.

My Christmas hopes are different now. I hope people addicted to drugs find treatment. I hope teens I know find good friends. I hope wars around the world end. I hope kids living in violent neighborhoods find safety and success in life.

John the Baptist had similar hopes. He lived in a land full of poverty and violence. He called people to change their lives by sharing their wealth and treating others fairly and kindly. He told them Jesus was coming to baptize them with the Holy Spirit and fire; in other words, Jesus would give them the courage and passion to hope and work for a better world.

John's words hold true today. Look around the world this Advent. Can your Christmas hopes focus on a better world? Can you ask Jesus for the courage and passion to go out to do your part?

Take :10 Reflect

If a word or phrase from the Gospel grabs your heart, sit quietly for several minutes, repeating it to yourself and asking God to show you how it applies to your life. Or, reflect and possibly journal on the following questions:

- What are the problems your community faces, and how can you start this Advent to make a difference?

Do the Unthinkable

Take :05 Examine

How did I live out last week's Gospel message? What was tough? What was rewarding?

Take :05 Read

Mary set out and traveled to the hill country in haste to a town of Judah, where she entered the house of Zechariah and greeted Elizabeth. When Elizabeth heard Mary's greeting, the infant leaped in her womb, and Elizabeth, filled with the Holy Spirit, cried out in a loud voice and said, "Blessed are you among women, and blessed is the fruit of your womb. And how does this happen to me, that the mother of my Lord should come to me? For at the moment the sound of your greeting reached my ears, the infant in my womb leaped for joy. Blessed are you who believed that what was spoken to you by the Lord would be fulfilled."

I recently read a story about a teen so upset about school policy that he ran for the school board to change things. He wasn't on the ballot. So he had to go door to door to ask people to write his name in. Victory was unthinkable, but he believed in his mission.

He won.

He reminds me of Mary. She was a teen when she was pregnant with Jesus. Her Jewish religion told her that God had not forgotten God's people, even though they suffered under Roman occupation. She grew up hearing the Hebrew Scriptures proclaim that God liberates God's people. Then

Gabriel's message to Mary challenged her to think the unthinkable—that she would bear the child who would bring God's liberating power into the world.

She believed.

In this week's Gospel, Elizabeth, Mary's relative and the mother of John the Baptist, calls Mary blessed, because she believed God's promises to her, as wild as they might seem to some. *Blessed* is another way to say that Mary was closely connected to God. That connection brought her a sense of confidence, purpose, and serenity. That connection brought us Jesus. Mary and the teen who ran for the school board believed and acted.

How about you? God's promises still seem unbelievable to many. Peace to all people. Enemies forgiving and reconciling. Justice for the poor. But those promises are fulfilled in our world when people like you and me do what others consider unthinkable. It seems crazy to forgive that person who disrespected you. But if you do it, God's promise is fulfilled. Why waste your time helping people with AIDS or being there for someone who is alone in a nursing home? Because if you do it, God's promise if fulfilled.

Be like Mary this Advent. Do the unthinkable, and you'll experience the sense of purpose, confidence, and serenity that comes with being blessed.

Take :10 Reflect

If a word or phrase from the Gospel grabs your heart, sit quietly for several minutes, repeating it to yourself and asking God to show you how it applies to your life. Or, reflect and possibly journal on the following question:

• What's something you could do this week that would be unthinkable to many but applauded by Mary?

No One Is Turned Away

Take :05 Examine

How did I live out last week's Gospel message? What was tough? What was rewarding?

Take :05 Read

When the angels went away from them to heaven, the shepherds said to one another, "Let us go, then, to Bethlehem to see this thing that has taken place, which the Lord has made known to us." So they went in haste and found Mary and Joseph, and the infant lying in the manger. When they saw this, they made known the message that had been told them about this child. All who heard it were amazed by what had been told them by the shepherds. And Mary kept all these things, reflecting on them in her heart. Then the shepherds returned, glorifying and praising God for all they had heard and seen, just as it had been told to them.

How would people react if you replaced the shepherds in your parish manger scene with statues of homeless people, AIDS patients, or lonely nursing home residents? I don't know how my fellow parishioners would react, but at least the scene would show who the angels might visit if Jesus were born today. They are some of our modern-day shepherds.

People in ancient Israel looked down on shepherds. They were seen as a low-class people, and many folks turned away from them. But they were the first ones, according to Luke, whom the angels told about Jesus' birth.

Why? Because God turns first toward those whom others turn away from. In fact, that is the power and beauty of Christmas. It shows God's deliberate choice to turn toward a broken world, especially toward the people who are most broken. In fact, God, through Jesus, embraces the people others try to avoid. God wants to be that close.

Jesus was born two thousand years ago. But the hope of Christmas becomes flesh and blood again today when we let God's spirit turn us toward those who suffer the most—our modern-day shepherds. People are walking the streets, feeling alone in school, eating in soup kitchens, dying in hospitals, and living forgotten in nursing homes, and those are the people whom God wants to turn toward and embrace. And God wants to do that through your love and actions.

You might need hope this season too. You'll find it if you remember God wants to turn toward the painful parts of your life and offer mercy, forgiveness, and peace. In fact, those are especially the parts of your life God wants to touch and heal. We all have problems, sinful habits, or worries that we're reluctant to deal with. Let God be born into those parts of your life by praying about them and maybe even talking to a minister about them.

Isn't it great? God always turns toward us, never away. Merry Christmas.

Take :10 Reflect

If a word or phrase from the Gospel grabs your heart, sit quietly for several minutes, repeating it to yourself and asking God to show you how it applies to your life. Or, reflect and possibly journal on the following questions:

- Who are the modern-day shepherds in your community? What are the parts of your life that you most need God to turn toward and heal this Christmas season?

Holy Families Are Far from Perfect

Take :05 Examine

How did I live out last week's Gospel message? What was tough? What was rewarding?

Take :05 Read

Each year Jesus' parents went to Jerusalem for the feast of Passover, and when he was twelve years old, they went up according to festival custom. After they had completed its days, as they were returning, the boy Jesus remained behind in Jerusalem, but his parents did not know it. Thinking that he was in the caravan, they journeyed for a day and looked for him among their relatives and acquaintances, but not finding him, they returned to Jerusalem to look for him. After three days they found him in the temple, sitting in the midst of the teachers, listening to them and asking them questions, and all who heard him were astounded at his understanding and his answers. When his parents saw him, they were astonished, and his mother said to him, "Son, why have you done this to us? Your father and I have been looking for you with great anxiety." And he said to them, "Why were you looking for me? Did you not know that I must be in my Father's house?" But they did not understand what he said to them. (Luke 2:41–50)

Let me tell you about three "holy families" I've known.

One struggled when the sixteen-year-old son developed a drinking problem. Another struggled on the edge of poverty but was usually the first to volunteer to help the poor. The third was a family of active parishioners headed by parents whose marriage ended in divorce.

None had a perfect family life with perfect relationships. But each was holy because its members had asked for God's help in their family struggles. Holy doesn't mean perfect.

Look at this week's Gospel. Jesus takes off without telling his parents. His parents seemingly don't understand him. Mary lashes out at Jesus when they find him. Jesus responds with what sounds like a smart remark. It would seem that *the* Holy Family wasn't a perfect family either.

Jesus grew up in a family that probably had its own share of conflicts and misunderstandings. But Jesus' family was holy because God was so much a part of family life. It was during a religious trip to Jerusalem that Jesus was lost.

The three families I mentioned earlier were holy too, for the same reasons. Each came to church for help when family members struggled, whether it was with addiction, poverty, or divorce. Whatever your family situation is—and there are many different kinds of families today—you can make your family more holy by involving God in your family relationships. Go to Mass with family. Encourage family members to pray and serve others together. Pray about family fights. Ask God's strength to forgive, or ask God for forgiveness. Talk to a minister when family problems seem overwhelming.

A holy family isn't a perfect family. So don't try to be perfect. Just do your best to be holy.

Take :10 Reflect

If a word or phrase from the Gospel grabs your heart, sit quietly for several minutes, repeating it to yourself and asking God to show you how it applies to your life. Or, reflect and possibly journal on the following question:

- What are three ways you could bring more holiness to your family life?

God Still Chooses "Marys" Today

Take :05 Examine

How did I live out last week's Gospel message? What was tough? What was rewarding?

Take :05 Read

The shepherds went in haste to Bethlehem and found Mary and Joseph, and the infant lying in the manger. When they saw this, they made known the message that had been told them about this child. All who heard it were amazed by what had been told them by the shepherds. And Mary kept all these things, reflecting on them in her heart. Then the shepherds returned, glorifying and praising God for all they had heard and seen, just as it had been told to them.

When eight days were completed for his circumcision, he was named Jesus, the name given him by the angel before he was conceived in the womb.

I don't remember her name, but I'll always remember her. She was one of my clients when I worked as a lawyer for low-income women. She was strong and courageous. Her husband was a homeless drug addict, so she raised their kids alone. She worked hard, but her job at a leather purse factory wouldn't guarantee her full-time work. She needed welfare to feed her two kids.

During her first day at the factory, someone cut off a finger running the machine she was learning to run. But she took the job anyway, even though she had no medical insurance. She also was an artist, her passion being sewing. She made the wedding dresses and prom dresses for all her nieces. She had a beautiful smile.

She needed my help because the state aid office had mistakenly cut her family's food stamps. But I think she helped me more. She taught me so much about personal self-confidence and endurance, about love and commitment to family, about faith in God. God worked through her to teach me. That would surprise a lot of people in our society, which often looks down upon single mothers on welfare.

God chooses the people our society would least expect to teach us valuable lessons. Mary, like the woman I just told you about, is a perfect example. She was a poor, unmarried, pregnant young woman in a society where women were treated like property, and adultery could end your life. Mary was a Jew from a rural area (Galilee) looked down upon by many elites in Jerusalem.

Yet it was Mary whom God favored. We now see her as the greatest disciple.

What does that say about the women looked down upon in our world today? Do you think we can learn from poor women struggling to feed their families? Might God be trying to teach us through women living in shelters or in countries torn by violence and poverty?

Those are all good questions to ponder as we spend time thinking about the mother of Jesus.

Take :10 Reflect

If a word or phrase from the Gospel grabs your heart, sit quietly for several minutes, repeating it to yourself and asking God to show you how it applies to your life. Or, reflect and possibly journal on the following question:

- Have you ever learned an important lesson about life from someone society looks down upon?

Modern-Day Magi

Take :05 Examine

How did I live out last week's Gospel message? What was tough? What was rewarding?

Take :05 Read

When Jesus was born in Bethlehem of Judea, in the days of King Herod, behold, magi from the east arrived in Jerusalem, saying, "Where is the newborn king of the Jews? We saw his star at its rising and have come to do him homage." When King Herod heard this, he was greatly troubled, and all Jerusalem with him. . . . Then Herod called the magi secretly and ascertained from them the time of the star's appearance. He sent them to Bethlehem and said, "Go and search diligently for the child. When you have found him, bring me word, that I too may go and do him homage." After their audience with the king they set out. And behold, the star that they had seen at its rising preced-ed them, until it came and stopped over the place where the child was. They were overjoyed at seeing the star, and on entering the house they saw the child with Mary his mother. They prostrated themselves and did him homage. Then they opened their treasures and offered him gifts of gold, frankin-cense, and myrrh. And having been warned in a dream not to return to Herod, they departed for their country by another way. (Matthew 2:1–3,7–12)

I have a Palestinian friend, a Muslim, who spent some years training young Palestinians that the Islamic faith calls them to work nonviolently in settling disputes. My friend came to the United States to study Catholicism so that he could return to Palestine and foster peace by teaching Muslims about Christians.

I see him as a wise man. He is letting God work through his life to spread God's message in a war-torn area. His courage and commitment inspire me. Through his commitment to Islam, I hear God calling me to greater Christian discipleship.

This week's Gospel about the Magi shows how the early Christians were challenged to recognize that God reaches out to people in every nation. God loves all people. The Israelites were God's Chosen People because God chose them to be an example to the world of faith and justice, not because God loved them more than any other people.

This is an important message for Catholics in the United States. Some Americans think the United States is God's favorite nation. They believe that almost everything the U.S. government does is God's will. Some find it hard to realize that God works in people throughout the world, even in people in non-Christian nations. We need to listen to voices from places like Palestine because God speaks to us through them. Our Church teaches that God is active in religions and nations around the world, not just ours. My friend, a devout Muslim working for peace, is a perfect example, a modern-day magi.

Take :10 Reflect

If a word or phrase from the Gospel grabs your heart, sit quietly for several minutes, repeating it to yourself and asking God to show you how it applies to your life. Or, reflect and possibly journal on the following questions:

- What do I admire about different religions, or what have I learned about God from people in different countries?

Baptism of the Lord
Luke 3:15–16,21–22

It's Good to Be "Claimed"

Take :05 Examine

How did I live out last week's Gospel message? What was tough? What was rewarding?

Take :05 Read

The people were filled with expectation, and all were asking in their hearts whether John might be the Christ. John answered them all, saying, "I am baptizing you with water, but one mightier than I is coming. I am not worthy to loosen the thongs of his sandals. He will baptize you with the Holy Spirit and fire."

After all the people had been baptized and Jesus also had been baptized and was praying, heaven was opened and the Holy Spirit descended upon him in bodily form like a dove. And a voice came from heaven, "You are my beloved Son; with you I am well pleased."

I see them each day I'm in a high school. They are the teens who always seem to be alone, walking with their heads down, rarely laughing with anyone.

I look for ways to show them they've been "claimed."

What do I mean? Each one of us has been claimed by God and God's love. The Gospel this week tells a story about Jesus realizing that God had claimed him as a son.

It's good to be claimed. If I'm claimed by God, God will always be close to strengthen and support me. If I'm claimed by God, God will show me a path toward a fulfilling life. If I'm claimed by God, God will call me back during those times when I turn away from God or when I feel like a failure.

I'm claimed by God, so everything *is* going to be okay, regardless of my worries, fears, or failures. When the world tries to distance me, I just need to stay focused on God's love for me.

Like God did with Jesus, God claimed us during our Baptism. Our Baptism, like Jesus' baptism, shows our core identity. We are children of God, the creator of the universe. And nothing can change that. Knowing that he was claimed by God, Jesus was free to act with courage, to stand up for the poor, to reach out to the unpopular, and to heal the sick people others feared.

Belonging to God can free you too, if you let it. It can free you from having to impress friends or foes. It can free you to be yourself and use your talents courageously to change the world.

But a lot of people, especially some teens, don't feel claimed by God, or by anyone. They live lonely, painful lives. That's why God needs us to remind them that God loves them as sons or daughters. We can do that by reaching out to the forgotten people in our society, by stopping people who put others down, by inviting people who seem friendless to join our circle of friends.

You've been claimed by God's love. Pass it on.

Take :10 Reflect

If a word or phrase from the Gospel grabs your heart, sit quietly for several minutes, repeating it to yourself and asking God to show you how it applies to your life. Or, reflect and possibly journal on the following questions:

- Who do you know who lives like they believe God's love will never leave them? Who do you know who needs to be reminded that they are loved?

Turn Some Water into Wine!

Take :05 Examine

How did I live out last week's Gospel message? What was
tough? What was rewarding?

Take :05 Read

*There was a wedding at Cana in Galilee, and the mother of
Jesus was there. Jesus and his disciples were also invited to the
wedding. When the wine ran short, the mother of Jesus said to
him, "They have no wine." And Jesus said to her, "Woman, how
does your concern affect me? My hour has not yet come." His
mother said to the servers, "Do whatever he tells you." Now
there were six stone water jars there for Jewish ceremonial
washings, each holding twenty to thirty gallons. Jesus told them,
"Fill the jars with water." So they filled them to the brim. Then he
told them, "Draw some out now and take it to the headwaiter."
So they took it. And when the headwaiter tasted the water that
had become wine, without knowing where it came from—
although the servers who had drawn the water knew—, the
headwaiter called the bridegroom and said to him, "Everyone
serves good wine first, and then when people have drunk freely,
an inferior one; but you have kept the good wine until now." Jesus
did this as the beginning of his signs at Cana in Galilee and so
revealed his glory, and his disciples began to believe in him.*

I'll always remember the day of the $25,000 anonymous
donation. A group of students and I were running our
school's weeklong hunger awareness campaign. It included
prayer services at school and a public plea for all people to

consider donating. Midway through the campaign's last day, the students and I were collecting donations in front of the school when the school president gave us the news—an anonymous donor had made a $25,000 donation. We were floored.

Then we realized that Jesus, who changed water into expensive wine, is still working incredible miracles.

That's the point of this week's Gospel. The Gospel writer crafted this story to show early Christians that Jesus' life was a sign of God's surprising, miraculous, overwhelming love. The story shows that Jesus' life began a new age that would reveal God's power in miraculous and dramatic ways.

We live in that new age. But God's power breaks into our world only when we let God work in our lives. We were shocked by our $25,000 donation, but I believe we received it because the student leaders let God use them to fight hunger, and the donor let God move him or her toward generosity.

Today that donation is in a bank. And student leaders still use the interest it earns to help families with emergency rent and medical bills. So the donation continues to be a sign of God's power in the world.

You can be too.

Take :10 Reflect

If a word or phrase from the Gospel grabs your heart, sit quietly for several minutes, repeating it to yourself and asking God to show you how it applies to your life. Or, reflect and possibly journal on the following questions:

- When have you been shocked by God's power in your life, or when have you seen another Christian accomplish something miraculous?

Jesus Has a Career for You

Take :05 Examine

How did I live out last week's Gospel message? What was tough? What was rewarding?

Take :05 Read

Jesus returned to Galilee in the power of the Spirit, and news of him spread throughout the whole region. He taught in their synagogues and was praised by all.

He came to Nazareth, where he had grown up, and went according to his custom into the synagogue on the sabbath day. He stood up to read and was handed a scroll of the prophet Isaiah. He unrolled the scroll and found the passage where it was written:

The Spirit of the Lord is upon me,
> because he has anointed me
> to bring glad tidings to the poor.
He has sent me to proclaim liberty to captives
> and recovery of sight to the blind,
> to let the oppressed go free,
> and to proclaim a year acceptable to the Lord.

Rolling up the scroll, he handed it back to the attendant and sat down, and the eyes of all in the synagogue looked intently at him. He said to them, "Today this Scripture passage is fulfilled in your hearing." (Luke 4:14–21)

I recently met some university students who made a year-long commitment to live together, pray together, and serve their community, all while taking their normal class loads.

These students aren't religion majors. They are studying for several different careers; nonetheless, they've decided to prepare at the same time for careers as disciples.

In this week's Gospel, Jesus announces his career. He will help the poor and challenge people to see what's really important in life. He will challenge religious laws and cure diseases that hold people captive. Unfortunately, I've met some Christians who admire Jesus but think his career is only for people who study theology, teach religious education, say Mass, or join religious orders.

That's why those university students inspired me. They realize that Jesus outlines every Christian's career in this Gospel, not just his own. In any career you'll see poor people who need help. You'll come across people who are blind to Christian values and need your example. And as United States citizens, you'll be called to vote for politicians who create laws and make economic decisions that can bring freedom or captivity to millions.

So be like the university students. Prepare now for your career as a disciple. You can't beat the retirement plan.

Take :10 Reflect

If a word or phrase from the Gospel grabs your heart, sit quietly for several minutes, repeating it to yourself and asking God to show you how it applies to your life. Or, reflect and possibly journal on the following question:

- Who is someone you know who isn't a religion teacher or professional minister but who inspires you by how actively he or she lives the Christian mission?

Don't Let Rejection Defeat You

Take :05 Examine

How did I live out last week's Gospel message? What was tough? What was rewarding?

Take :05 Read

Jesus began speaking in the synagogue, saying: "Today this Scripture passage is fulfilled in your hearing." And all spoke highly of him and were amazed at the gracious words that came from his mouth. They also asked, "Isn't this the son of Joseph?" He said to them, "Surely you will quote me this proverb, 'Physician, cure yourself,' and say, 'Do here in your native place the things that we heard were done in Capernaum.'" And he said, "Amen, I say to you, no prophet is accepted in his own native place. Indeed, I tell you, there were many widows in Israel in the days of Elijah when the sky was closed for three and a half years and a severe famine spread over the entire land. It was to none of these that Elijah was sent, but only to a widow in Zarephath in the land of Sidon. Again, there were many lepers in Israel during the time of Elisha the prophet; yet not one of them was cleansed, but only Naaman the Syrian." When the people in the synagogue heard this, they were all filled with fury. They rose up, drove him out of the town, and led him to the brow of the hill on which their town had been built, to hurl him down headlong. But Jesus passed through the midst of them and went away.

Christianity is risky business.

Remember last week's Gospel? Jesus announced his life's mission in his home synagogue. The story continues this week when he tells his neighbors that he can't work miracles for them because their minds are closed to his message. That spurs them to attack.

Sometimes we minimize the risks that come with a Christian life. This Gospel warns us not to. When we follow Jesus' lifestyle, we likely will face rejection. Sometimes that rejection even comes from the people who know us best. I know some teens that have had conflicts with friends because they stopped some sinful, but popular, behavior—like getting drunk. I know teens that have served the poor and then faced conflicts because they defended the poor when friends or family called poor people lazy bums.

Rejection hurts whether you are young or old. It really hurts when people you care about put you down when you are just trying to do something good. It can tempt you to just make yourself fit in and walk away from Jesus' message.

That's why Christians need support from one another. Talk with other Christians when you face rejection. Call a friend. See an adult minister. Most Christians have faced rejection too and will want to help you through it.

It's also important to pray for strength and comfort when you face rejection. Remember, the person listening to your prayers was once rejected by the people of his own hometown.

Take :10 Reflect

If a word or phrase from the Gospel grabs your heart, sit quietly for several minutes, repeating it to yourself and asking God to show you how it applies to your life. Or, reflect and possibly journal on the following question:

- When have you faced rejection for making a Christian decision, and how did you deal with it?

Let God's Power Stun You Too

Take :05 Examine

How did I live out last week's Gospel message? What was tough? What was rewarding?

Take :05 Read

While the crowd was pressing in on Jesus and listening to the word of God, he was standing by the Lake of Gennesaret. He saw two boats there alongside the lake; the fishermen had disembarked and were washing their nets. Getting into one of the boats, the one belonging to Simon, he asked him to put out a short distance from the shore. Then he sat down and taught the crowds from the boat. After he had finished speaking, he said to Simon, "Put out into deep water and lower your nets for a catch." Simon said in reply, "Master, we have worked hard all night and have caught nothing, but at your command I will lower the nets." When they had done this, they caught a great number of fish and their nets were tearing. They signaled to their partners in the other boat to come to help them. They came and filled both boats so that the boats were in danger of sinking. When Simon Peter saw this, he fell at the knees of Jesus and said, "Depart from me, Lord, for I am a sinful man." For astonishment at the catch of fish they had made seized him and all those with him, and likewise James and John, the sons of Zebedee, who were partners of Simon. Jesus said to Simon, "Do not be afraid; from now on you will be catching men." When they brought their boats to the shore, they left everything and followed him.

I know Christians who worked hard to prevent the last United States–Iraq war. Before the war they split their time between the two countries, helping people there and trying to convince people here to avoid war. When the war started, some stayed in Iraq, where they comforted people during bombing raids and then peacefully welcomed U.S. troops when they arrived.

When I think of those people, I feel like Peter in this week's Gospel—humbled and awed. They showed me that God still inspires people to heroically reshape this world into God's Kingdom. I want God to work like that through me too.

That's the point of Luke's story this week. Peter, James, and John had fished all night without success. They were frustrated. They lowered their nets one more time to humor Jesus. You know the rest. Inspired by Jesus' power, they dropped everything and followed him.

Like Peter, we can get tired and frustrated, especially hearing all the bad news in the world. But God *is* working miracles each day. We need only to look around. Keep your eyes open for people doing good things, big and small, in your family, school, or community. Let those examples show you God's love for the world. Let them remind you that you can work miracles too.

Then drop everything and follow the Master who calls us to be fishers of people.

Take :10 Reflect

If a word or phrase from the Gospel grabs your heart, sit quietly for several minutes, repeating it to yourself and asking God to show you how it applies to your life. Or, reflect and possibly journal on the following question:

- Who do you know that shows God's love and power through acts of kindness, courage, or charity?

Does God Play Favorites?

Take :05 Examine

How did I live out last week's Gospel message? What was tough? What was rewarding?

Take :05 Read

Jesus came down with the Twelve and stood on a stretch of level ground with a great crowd of his disciples and a large number of the people from all Judea and Jerusalem and the coastal region of Tyre and Sidon. And raising his eyes toward his disciples he said:

"Blessed are you who are poor,
for the kingdom of God is yours.
Blessed are you who are now hungry,
for you will be satisfied.
Blessed are you who are now weeping,
for you will laugh.
Blessed are you when people hate you,
and when they exclude and insult you,
and denounce your name as evil
on account of the Son of Man.

Rejoice and leap for joy on that day! Behold, your reward will be great in heaven. For their ancestors treated the prophets in the same way.

But woe to you who are rich,
for you have received your consolation.
Woe to you who are filled now,
for you will be hungry.
Woe to you who laugh now,
for you will grieve and weep.
Woe to you when all speak well of you,
for their ancestors treated the false
prophets in this way."

One of the biggest challenges I face in working with high school students is to never play favorites. It's tough. I'm human. So naturally I like some students more than others. But I work hard to avoid giving certain students special rights or doing special favors for particular students.

God sees things differently. And Luke's Gospel this week tells us who God's favorites are: the people who are poor, who mourn, who face persecution for doing the right thing. Sure, God loves everyone equally, but the Scriptures show time and again that God's actions favor the powerless and people who suffer. We know that because God continually sends people—like Moses and Jesus—to help them.

Blessed in this Gospel means "favored." Jesus tells his disciples that God is working to construct a world that favors the powerless. God's Reign will change things so that the people on the bottom will have what they need. That's bad news, he says, to people who abuse power, don't share wealth, or cause others pain.

Jesus favored people without power by hanging out with them, eating with them, and challenging customs that caused them to suffer. We need to take our cue from him by giving people who suffer the highest priority in our lives. We show God's favor to those who are powerless by serving them, learning from them, and working for a just society. We show God's favor to people who mourn by comforting them. By doing these things, we also show people who abuse power, horde power, or hurt others that it's time to change.

Take :10 Reflect

If a word or phrase from the Gospel grabs your heart, sit quietly for several minutes, repeating it to yourself and asking God to show you how it applies to your life. Or, reflect and possibly journal on the following question:

*   Who inspires you by how they favor poor people or those who mourn?

Be Tough Like Jesus

Take :05 Examine

How did I live out last week's Gospel message? What was tough? What was rewarding?

Take :05 Read

Jesus said to his disciples: "To you who hear I say, love your enemies, do good to those who hate you, bless those who curse you, pray for those who mistreat you. To the person who strikes you on one cheek, offer the other one as well, and from the person who takes your cloak, do not withhold even your tunic. Give to everyone who asks of you, and from the one who takes what is yours do not demand it back. Do to others as you would have them do to you. For if you love those who love you, what credit is that to you? Even sinners love those who love them. And if you do good to those who do good to you, what credit is that to you? Even sinners do the same. If you lend money to those from whom you expect repayment, what credit is that to you? Even sinners lend to sinners, and get back the same amount. But rather, love your enemies and do good to them, and lend expecting nothing back; then your reward will be great and you will be children of the Most High, for he himself is kind to the ungrateful and the wicked. Be merciful, just as your Father is merciful.

"Stop judging and you will not be judged. Stop condemning and you will not be condemned. Forgive and you will be forgiven. Give, and gifts will be given to you; a good measure, packed together, shaken down, and overflowing, will be poured into your lap. For the measure with which you measure will in return be measured out to you."

This is the passage we'd like to ignore. Love your enemy. Turn the other cheek. "No way!" part of us screams.

Dr. Martin Luther King Jr. would disagree.

During the 1960s civil rights marches, black protestors faced police who attacked them with clubs and dogs. Their homes were bombed. Some were lynched. But through it all, Doctor King insisted that blacks could win their rights only by following this week's Gospel passage.

Jesus calls us to *love* our enemies, not *like* them. We love someone when we act for his or her best interests—regardless of our feelings. Jesus also says turn the other cheek. But that doesn't mean run. He doesn't say back down. Rather, he challenges us to find a nonviolent way to stand up for our rights.

These commands are tough to follow when you face people who put you down or threaten you. But you can do it through prayer and practice. You also need support from fellow Christians.

Jesus followed these commands. Look at the difference he made. You can change your world too by following his example. Doctor King's supporters refused to fight or hate when they were attacked. Instead, they often prayed and sang Gospel songs. That might sound crazy, but their courage inspired others to join them, changed some people's minds about them, won their rights, and saved a lot of bloodshed.

Take :10 Reflect

If a word or phrase from the Gospel grabs your heart, sit quietly for several minutes, repeating it to yourself and asking God to show you how it applies to your life. Or, reflect and possibly journal on the following question:

- What are some practical ways teens can show love toward enemies and "turn the other cheek" when they feel attacked?

Yank Out That Beam

Take :05 Examine

How did I live out last week's Gospel message? What was tough? What was rewarding?

Take :05 Read

Jesus told his disciples a parable, "Can a blind person guide a blind person? Will not both fall into a pit? No disciple is superior to the teacher; but when fully trained, every disciple will be like his teacher. Why do you notice the splinter in your brother's eye, but do not perceive the wooden beam in your own? How can you say to your brother, 'Brother, let me remove that splinter in your eye,' when you do not even notice the wooden beam in your own eye? You hypocrite! Remove the wooden beam from your eye first; then you will see clearly to remove the splinter in your brother's eye.

"A good tree does not bear rotten fruit, nor does a rotten tree bear good fruit. For every tree is known by its own fruit. For people do not pick figs from thornbushes, nor do they gather grapes from brambles. A good person out of the store of goodness in his heart produces good, but an evil person out of a store of evil produces evil; for from the fullness of the heart the mouth speaks."

I have a friend recovering from alcoholism and drug addiction. He has spent time in prison because of his addictions. And his life inspires me.

What inspires me is the gut-wrenching honesty he shows about his personal flaws. When he has a conflict with someone, he first looks at whether he did something wrong.

He always apologizes when he realizes that he caused or worsened a conflict by his attitude or comments.

I wish I could be more like him. For some reason it's hard for humans to look honestly at ourselves, especially when we are fighting with someone. It is much easier to blame or judge other people. But that's exactly what Jesus warns against in this week's Gospel. Christians need gut-wrenching honesty about themselves. The more we look at our faults—knowing God loves us despite them—the more we mature and our faults no longer control us. Then we can discover our full potential.

My friend says he can continue to recover from addiction only if he remains honest about all his weaknesses, especially his desire for drugs and alcohol. That self-honesty, he says, frees him daily to grow, change, and contribute to the world in powerful ways.

You can follow my friend's example. Each night take time to look honestly at yourself. Look at your strengths and weaknesses. Be proud of the good things you did during the day. But own up to your mistakes, and ask God to help you learn from them. Over time you'll develop a habit for gut-wrenching honesty, and with that will come pride, maturity, and the respect of the people who know you.

Take :10 Reflect

If a word or phrase from the Gospel grabs your heart, sit quietly for several minutes, repeating it to yourself and asking God to show you how it applies to your life. Or, reflect and possibly journal on the following questions:

- When you look honestly at yourself, what are your greatest strengths? When you look honestly at yourself, what are your greatest weaknesses? Can you turn your weaknesses over to God?

What's Tempting *You?*

Take :05 Examine

How did I live out last week's Gospel message? What was tough? What was rewarding?

Take :05 Read

Filled with the Holy Spirit, Jesus returned from the Jordan and was led by the Spirit into the desert for forty days, to be tempted by the devil. He ate nothing during those days, and when they were over he was hungry. The devil said to him, "If you are the Son of God, command this stone to become bread." Jesus answered him, "It is written, One does not live on bread alone." *Then he took him up and showed him all the kingdoms of the world in a single instant. The devil said to him, "I shall give to you all this power and glory; for it has been handed over to me, and I may give it to whomever I wish. All this will be yours, if you worship me." Jesus said to him in reply, "It is written:*

You shall worship the Lord, your God,
    and him alone shall you serve."
Then he led him to Jerusalem, made him stand on the parapet of the temple, and said to him, "If you are the Son of God, throw yourself down from here, for it is written:

He will command his angels concerning you, to guard
        you,
and:

With their hands they will support you,
    lest you dash your foot against a stone."
Jesus said to him in reply, "It also says,

You shall not put the Lord, your God, to the test."
When the devil had finished every temptation, he departed from him for a time.

I have been amazed at some stories about millionaire executives who swindle their companies to get even richer. How could money be so tempting, especially to rich people? Riches have just never tempted me.

But I face other temptations. I ask God daily for strength because I am tempted daily to sin in ways that hurt others and hold me back from being everything I can be.

The Gospel this week shows Jesus struggling with temptation. A born leader, he was tempted to abuse his power. Many people in Israel were waiting for a *messiah*—a word we understand as *savior*—to lead a violent revolt against Rome. But he knew God called him to greater things.

How about you? Each person faces different temptations. What tempts you to be selfish and tempts you away from doing great things for God? Lent is the time to explore that question in your soul, to see where you've surrendered to temptation and where you need God's strength to resist those temptations.

Here's an idea: List your six greatest temptations and then reflect on one each week during Lent. Remember times you gave in. Remember times you resisted. Brainstorm ways to avoid the particular temptation you're focusing on. Look at what the Bible says about it. Ask God for the vision to see the temptation clearly the next time you face it and for the strength to resist it.

Take :10 Reflect

If a word or phrase from the Gospel grabs your heart, sit quietly for several minutes, repeating it to yourself and asking God to show you how it applies to your life. Or, reflect and possibly journal on the following questions:

- When has giving in to a temptation hurt you? How does giving in to a temptation keep you from being the person you think God wants you to be?

Do You Pray or Escape?

Take :05 Examine

How did I live out last week's Gospel message? What was tough? What was rewarding?

Take :05 Read

Jesus took Peter, John, and James and went up the mountain to pray. While he was praying his face changed in appearance and his clothing became dazzling white. And behold, two men were conversing with him, Moses and Elijah, who appeared in glory and spoke of his exodus that he was going to accomplish in Jerusalem. Peter and his companions had been overcome by sleep, but becoming fully awake, they saw his glory and the two men standing with him. As they were about to part from him, Peter said to Jesus, "Master, it is good that we are here; let us make three tents, one for you, one for Moses, and one for Elijah." But he did not know what he was saying. While he was still speaking, a cloud came and cast a shadow over them, and they became frightened when they entered the cloud. Then from the cloud came a voice that said, "This is my chosen Son; listen to him." After the voice had spoken, Jesus was found alone. They fell silent and did not at that time tell anyone what they had seen.

It happens pretty regularly at the end of powerful youth-group prayer meetings and retreats: No one wants to leave. So many times teens have told me how sad they feel about having to go back to the real world.

Peter feels the same way in this week's Gospel. The Transfiguration baffles many people. But just think of it this way: Jesus and his closest friends go up a mountain and pray, and during their prayer they realize the importance of Jesus and his mission. They connect his mission to historic religious leaders like Moses and Elijah. They feel God's presence. Peter wants to stay.

But maybe the most important part of the story is the end. They go back down the mountain and head toward Jerusalem, where their insights will change how they live in the real world. We know how the story ends.

Here's the lesson for us. Our prayer life isn't for us. It is for our journey in the world, where God calls us to live the Reign's values. That doesn't mean prayer shouldn't comfort us when we struggle with personal problems. It should. But youth-group meetings, retreats, and personal quiet time with Jesus must also turn our focus toward friends and family who need our support, poor people who need our compassion, and society's injustices that need our activism. Our prayer life should help us be Christ's presence to all people—from the people in our schools to the people in faraway lands. If our prayer life doesn't do this, then prayer is little more than an escape from reality.

Lent is a good time to evaluate your prayer and worship life. Is it an escape or a fueling station for your journey as a disciple?

Take :10 Reflect

If a word or phrase from the Gospel grabs your heart, sit quietly for several minutes, repeating it to yourself and asking God to show you how it applies to your life. Or, reflect and possibly journal on the following question:

- What prayer or worship experience has challenged you and strengthened you to make a Christian decision in the real world?

Add Some Fertilizer to Your Life This Lent

Take :05 Examine

How did I live out last week's Gospel message? What was tough? What was rewarding?

Take :05 Read

Some people told Jesus about the Galileans whose blood Pilate had mingled with the blood of their sacrifices. Jesus said to them in reply, "Do you think that because these Galileans suffered in this way they were greater sinners than all other Galileans? By no means! But I tell you, if you do not repent, you will all perish as they did! Or those eighteen people who were killed when the tower at Siloam fell on them—do you think they were more guilty than everyone else who lived in Jerusalem? By no means! But I tell you, if you do not repent, you will all perish as they did!"

And he told them this parable: "There once was a person who had a fig tree planted in his orchard, and when he came in search of fruit on it but found none, he said to the gardener, 'For three years now I have come in search of fruit on this fig tree but have found none. So cut it down. Why should it exhaust the soil?' He said to him in reply, 'Sir, leave it for this year also, and I shall cultivate the ground around it and fertilize it; it may bear fruit in the future. If not you can cut it down.'"

I have a priest friend who never gives up on people. He worked for some time in Chicago's inner city and even let homeless gang members live with him while they put their lives back together. Those kids had lived tough lives and had done some bad things, but my friend was always able to see their potential and, regardless of the mistakes they had made, worked hard to help them develop it.

That's the point of Jesus' fig-tree parable. God is the patient gardener, advising the landowner against cutting down the tree. He promises to fertilize it. Give it time, he says. It just needs a little help.

It's nice to know that's how God deals with us. Too often I give up on people. I think they can't change. Or, I look at how hard it is for me to change sinful habits and I want to give up on myself. During those times Penance and Reconciliation with a priest I trust can be good for me. The sacrament reminds me about God's patience with me and God's willingness to "fertilize" me so that I grow. God fertilizes us through prayer, Mass, service, and friends with similar values. Penance and Reconciliation also reminds me to show God's mercy to others. Finally, it often reminds me that I can fertilize the lives of others by listening and caring about them without judgment, as well as by challenging their behavior lovingly when they are on the wrong track.

Lent is a good time to add some fertilizer to your life. And celebrating Penance and Reconciliation can be a great gardening technique.

Take :10 Reflect

If a word or phrase from the Gospel grabs your heart, sit quietly for several minutes, repeating it to yourself and asking God to show you how it applies to your life. Or, reflect and possibly journal on the following question:

- How could an honest conversation about life with a priest or another minister help a teen grow?

Fourth Sunday of Lent
Luke 15:1–3, 11–32

Come Home

Take :05 Examine

How did I live out last week's Gospel message? What was tough? What was rewarding?

Take :05 Read

"But now we must celebrate and rejoice, because your brother was dead and has come to life again; he was lost and has been found." (Luke 15:32)

(*Note:* Because of the length of this week's Gospel, "The Prodigal Son," I have included only the last verse here. Please look up the Gospel in a Bible and read it in its entirety before reading the following reflection.)

Take a moment to look at your fingerprint. Experts say it is unique. You share it with no one who lives or has ever lived. Let it remind you that God wanted you, specifically you, to come into this world. And let it remind you that our loving God grieves for you, specifically you, when you hurt, and misses you, specifically you, when you turn away.

Let this week's Gospel dispel all the false views of God you may have heard. God is not angry or vengeful when we sin. God is not an accountant who tallies our sins against our good deeds or a cop who waits to punish us when we err. Unfortunately, many people hold on to those images. Some ministers even teach them, often because they misunderstand Old Testament Scripture passages that seem to portray God as angry or vengeful.

Jesus tried to dispel those images of God as he announced the beginning of God's Reign. "Rejoice," he said. Our loving Father is running to greet us right now. Turn toward God and let God embrace you.

Look at the lost son in the Gospel story this week. He basically had wished his father dead by asking for his inheritance. But when he returns because he has nowhere else to go, the father runs to him, gives him the family ring, clothes him in the best robe, and kills a fattened calf (people ate meat rarely). If you read the text closely, you see that the father doesn't even let his son complete his apology before ordering all this.

Lent is time to come home. We all stray. We live in a world that often calls us away from God. But God knows each of us by our fingerprint, knows when we turn away, and still always stands waiting, scanning the horizon, maybe weeping, hoping to see us turn back, looking for a chance to run toward us and embrace us once again.

Take :10 Reflect

If a word or phrase from the Gospel grabs your heart, sit quietly for several minutes, repeating it to yourself and asking God to show you how it applies to your life. Or, reflect and possibly journal on the following question:

- In what ways do you need to come home to God this Lent?

Care About People—Don't Use Them

Take :05 Examine

How did I live out last week's Gospel message? What was tough? What was rewarding?

Take :05 Read

Jesus went to the Mount of Olives. But early in the morning he arrived again in the temple area, and all the people started coming to him, and he sat down and taught them. Then the scribes and the Pharisees brought a woman who had been caught in adultery and made her stand in the middle. They said to him, "Teacher, this woman was caught in the very act of committing adultery. Now in the law, Moses commanded us to stone such women. So what do you say?" They said this to test him, so that they could have some charge to bring against him. Jesus bent down and began to write on the ground with his finger. But when they continued asking him, he straightened up and said to them, "Let the one among you who is without sin be the first to throw a stone at her." Again he bent down and wrote on the ground. And in response, they went away one by one, beginning with the elders. So he was left alone with the woman before him. Then Jesus straightened up and said to her, "Woman, where are they? Has no one condemned you?" She replied, "No one, sir." Then Jesus said, "Neither do I condemn you. Go, and from now on do not sin any more."

The way I treated Bill is, unfortunately, a perfect example of how different I am from Jesus.

I worked with Bill many years ago at a newspaper. We were both reporters. Bill was always friendly, but his clothes were often rumpled and looked old. I made fun of him behind his back, using him to make myself more popular. Bill probably needed a friend and some understanding, but I never spent time getting to know him or care about him.

Jesus was so much different. He shows that in this week's Gospel. His opponents drag a woman caught in adultery before him. Why? They want to trap him, hoping he'll speak against Jewish religious law. They care nothing about the woman, her embarrassment, or why she sinned. Maybe she's not as guilty as she appears. They simply use her. Jesus, on the other hand, focuses on the woman. He ignores their question and acts with compassion toward her.

All of us have probably hurt people by using them. Some people use others for humor. Some for sex. Some for a grade or a promotion. Sometimes people let themselves be used, especially lonely people who crave attention. We've seen this happen in school, right? Pornography and prostitution also thrive because people let themselves be used and degraded.

It's sinful to use people, even when they agree to it. Lent is a good time to ask difficult questions. Have we used people? Do we have the courage of Jesus to stand up and stop others when we see them using people?

Take :10 Reflect

If a word or phrase from the Gospel grabs your heart, sit quietly for several minutes, repeating it to yourself and asking God to show you how it applies to your life. Or, reflect and possibly journal on the following question:

- When have you used someone else or stopped someone from being used?

It's Not the Persecution—
It's the Response

Take :05 Examine

How did I live out last week's Gospel message? What was
tough? What was rewarding?

Take :05 Read

*It was now about noon and darkness came over the whole land
until three in the afternoon because of an eclipse of the sun.
Then the veil of the temple was torn down the middle. Jesus
cried out in a loud voice, "Father, into your hands I commend my
spirit"; and when he had said this he breathed his last. The
centurion who witnessed what had happened glorified God and
said, "This man was innocent beyond doubt." (Luke 23:44–47)*

For several years I attended a unique Good Friday service
in Chicago. It was a prayer walk through downtown. At
several stops along the way, we listened while speakers
talked about places in our world where people still experi-
enced suffering and death. They talked about how poverty
strips people of their dignity, about governments that use
torture to destroy people's spirit, and about the countless
people each year who face execution.

You know, the "Passion" really started a long time before
Jesus. It started the first time in history one person perse-
cuted another. And it has continued without pause since
Jesus himself suffered and died.

So where can we find hope if history seems so filled
with pain and persecution? We can find hope in the Passion

of Jesus. Ultimately, Jesus' Passion isn't about suffering and persecution. The Passion is about Jesus' response.

Focus this Holy Week on Jesus' response to the people in his life—those who love him and those who reject him. He was fully human. Many scholars argue that Jesus didn't know he would be resurrected. Just like us, Jesus did not have complete certainty about what would happen to him after his death.

So watch this man during Holy Week. Despite his fear, uncertainty, and agony, he focuses on God and others. Through God's power he offers the last hours of his life as a lesson for how his friends and followers can find meaning in every hour of their lives.

Then focus on today's world. Yes, Jesus' Passion continues. But focus on how God's power still inspires people to be courageous. Scan the newspapers; you will find stories about people throughout the world who brave persecution and suffering to help others. Look around your school, church, or family; you will see people who sacrifice their lives for others. Go to a nursing home or hospital; you will meet people who still love despite tremendous suffering.

Jesus' death was not that unusual. Our world has been filled with suffering and pain since the first human beings made their appearance. But Jesus' response was unusual. His response made God's power even more available for Christians who seek to respond like him. And history is filled with those heroes.

Will you join their number?

Take :10 Reflect

If a word or phrase from the Gospel grabs your heart, sit quietly for several minutes, repeating it to yourself and asking God to show you how it applies to your life. Or, reflect and possibly journal on the following question:

- Who in your life responds to pain or persecution with the same love, courage, and faith that Jesus had in his last hours?

Enter Your Tomb

Take :05 Examine

How did I live out last week's Gospel message? What was tough? What was rewarding?

Take :05 Read

On the first day of the week, Mary of Magdala came to the tomb early in the morning, while it was still dark, and saw the stone removed from the tomb. So she ran and went to Simon Peter and to the other disciple whom Jesus loved, and told them, "They have taken the Lord from the tomb, and we don't know where they put him." So Peter and the other disciple went out and came to the tomb. They both ran, but the other disciple ran faster than Peter and arrived at the tomb first; he bent down and saw the burial cloths there, but did not go in. When Simon Peter arrived after him, he went into the tomb and saw the burial cloths there, and the cloth that had covered his head, not with the burial cloths but rolled up in a separate place. Then the other disciple also went in, the one who had arrived at the tomb first, and he saw and believed. For they did not yet understand the Scripture that he had to rise from the dead.

I have a friend who suffered abuse as a child. As an adult, the abuse caused problems for her relationships. It also led her to self-destructive behavior, like addiction and promiscuity.

But then she entered her "tomb" and found that God wanted to raise her like he raised Jesus.

We all live with tombs, where parts of us have died. Memories of being hurt. Memories of hurting others. Self-destructive behaviors. Our world has tombs too. Pockets of war and poverty. Nursing homes or hospitals where the old and sick lie alone.

But God removed the rock from Jesus' tomb and raised him. By doing that, God told all humanity that there is new life after the painful things we have suffered through. But you have to enter the tomb to see and believe.

We do that by facing our painful memories and mistakes. We allow ourselves to cry when recalling how we've been hurt instead of gutting it out. We apologize instead of being proud. We also do that by facing our world's pain. We turn toward the people and places that many people ignore because they are afraid or too busy. We turn toward them whether they live in our homes or in different countries.

But we don't have to enter these tombs alone. We can bring God's power with us. We bring it when we pray or seek guidance from the Scriptures about our painful memories or mistakes. We bring it when we seek help from friends, family, or counselors. We bring it when we respond to our world's pain with Jesus' compassion and nonviolence.

My friend entered her tomb. She sought help from counselors and her faith to face the abuse she suffered. As a result, she is now a stronger and happier person who makes a real difference in the lives of others.

Once again, God rolled back the stone and raised someone to new life. Jesus' Resurrection was only the beginning. I've seen and I believe.

Take :10 Reflect

If a word or phrase from the Gospel grabs your heart, sit quietly for several minutes, repeating it to yourself and asking God to show you how it applies to your life. Or, reflect and possibly journal on the following question:

- What tomb or tombs in your life or in the world do you need to enter with God?

Thomas Is Looking for You

Take :05 Examine

How did I live out last week's Gospel message? What was tough? What was rewarding?

Take :05 Read

On the evening of that first day of the week, when the doors were locked, where the disciples were, for fear of the Jews, Jesus came and stood in their midst and said to them, "Peace be with you. . . ."

Thomas, called Didymus, one of the Twelve, was not with them when Jesus came. So the other disciples said to him, "We have seen the Lord." But he said to them, "Unless I see the mark of the nails in his hands and put my finger into the nailmarks and put my hand into his side, I will not believe."

Now a week later his disciples were again inside and Thomas was with them. Jesus came, although the doors were locked, and stood in their midst and said, "Peace be with you." Then he said to Thomas, "Put your finger here and see my hands, and bring your hand and put it into my side, and do not be unbelieving, but believe." Thomas answered and said to him, "My Lord and my God!" Jesus said to him, "Have you come to believe because you have seen me? Blessed are those who have not seen and have believed."

Now Jesus did many other signs in the presence of his disciples that are not written in this book. But these are written that you may come to believe that Jesus is the Christ, the Son of God, and that through this belief you may have life in his name.
(John 20:19,24–31)

Someone once asked Gandhi, the great Hindu peacemaker, why he had rejected Christianity. Gandhi said he never rejected Jesus. He just couldn't find many Christians that actually lived like Jesus taught.

What would Gandhi say if he visited your church, family, youth group, or Catholic high school?

This week's Gospel points out an important reality about Jesus' Resurrection. People often need some proof to really believe in it. Thomas was like you and me. He found the disciples' story hard to believe until Jesus appeared and showed him his wounds.

Looking back on my life, I realize I became convinced about Jesus' victory over death because of Catholic heroes. I've come to believe because, like Thomas, I've seen Jesus' wounds in people like Oscar Romero, a Central-American bishop who was martyred because he protested oppression. I see Jesus' wounds in every person who sacrifices time, sweat, or blood to ease suffering or stand for good.

This Easter season ask yourself whether a doubting Thomas could see the resurrected Jesus in your daily life. Could someone come to believe in Christ by watching how you treat family, friends, and classmates? Would someone praise God because of how you sacrifice for the poor? Would someone believe the Gospel's message because of how you take risks to do the right thing?

If Gandhi followed you for a week, what would he say?

Take :10 Reflect

If a word or phrase from the Gospel grabs your heart, sit quietly for several minutes, repeating it to yourself and asking God to show you how it applies to your life. Or, reflect and possibly journal on the following question:

• What people in your life show you Jesus' wounds?

Your Mistakes Can Be "Food" for Others

Take :05 Examine

How did I live out last week's Gospel message? What was tough? What was rewarding?

Take :05 Read

This was now the third time Jesus was revealed to his disciples after being raised from the dead.

When they had finished breakfast, Jesus said to Simon Peter, "Simon, son of John, do you love me more than these?" Simon Peter answered him, "Yes, Lord, you know that I love you." Jesus said to him, "Feed my lambs." He then said to Simon Peter a second time, "Simon, son of John, do you love me?" Simon Peter answered him, "Yes, Lord, you know that I love you." Jesus said to him, "Tend my sheep." Jesus said to him the third time, "Simon, son of John, do you love me?" Peter was distressed that Jesus had said to him a third time, "Do you love me?" and he said to him, "Lord, you know everything; you know that I love you." Jesus said to him, "Feed my sheep. Amen, amen, I say to you, when you were younger, you used to dress yourself and go where you wanted; but when you grow old, you will stretch out your hands, and someone else will dress you and lead you where you do not want to go." He said this signifying by what kind of death he would glorify God. And when he had said this, he said to him, "Follow me." (John 21:14–19)

Sometimes I feel like Peter. Not because I'm holy, but because Jesus has given me the chance to admit my past mistakes, correct them, and use them for building God's Reign.

As a college student, I stopped going to church and praying. I lived a self-centered life. I didn't care about anyone but myself. Over time that lifestyle left me with a deep sense of emptiness. Jesus filled that emptiness when I turned back to God, sought forgiveness, and resolved to live differently. I'm still a sinner. But now I encourage young people to draw close to Christ and thus avoid the mistakes I made. I try to use my past mistakes to help others.

Jesus offers Peter that same opportunity in this week's Gospel. Peter denied Jesus three times. So Jesus invites Peter to repent and be forgiven by expressing his love three times. Peter has the chance to repair the damage his denials caused. Repentance can free you from the guilt that keeps you from fully loving yourself and others. You can't really be free until, like Peter, you try to correct the damage your sins leave behind.

You can also use those sins to help others. Look at how the Gospel uses Peter's sin to teach us about Jesus' love and our ability to start anew.

Easter is a good time to correct and learn from your mistakes. The Risen Christ offers you the opportunity and the courage to look honestly at your mistakes, repair damage they caused in your relationships, and use what you have learned to help others. Take up Christ on this offer. And then follow him.

Take :10 Reflect

If a word or phrase from the Gospel grabs your heart, sit quietly for several minutes, repeating it to yourself and asking God to show you how it applies to your life. Or, reflect and possibly journal on the following question:

- What places in your life are messy because of sin and need cleaning up this Easter?

You're in Good Hands

Take :05 Examine

How did I live out last week's Gospel message? What was tough? What was rewarding?

Take :05 Read

Jesus said: "My sheep hear my voice; I know them, and they follow me. I give them eternal life, and they shall never perish. No one can take them out of my hand. My Father, who has given them to me, is greater than all, and no one can take them out of the Father's hand. The Father and I are one."

There was an insurance company commercial running for many years that assured people they were "in good hands" with the company's policies.

Security. Insurance. Protection. At some level, isn't that what we all are looking for?

I worry about young people today because I've seen so many stressed out because they think that security comes only from becoming the smartest, the richest, the most popular, or the most athletic. They work or worry all day and night for their goals. And the stress takes a toll on them. Some get sick. Some start using drugs or alcohol. Some get involved with gangs. Some have problems with friends or family.

I wish they would all read this week's Gospel over and over. It is clear. We're in good hands—God's hands. And nothing can change that. We can't flunk out of God's hands. We can't get cut from or kicked out of God's hands. You need not be rich or popular to be in God's hands. Why do we worry so?

We can have an eternal life of meaning and love starting right now if we just recognize where we live—in God's hands. Who is this God? Ignore false images of God as judgmental and punishing. Jesus says he and God are one. So look at Jesus to understand God. You'll be reminded that God is a loving, merciful, and compassionate parent who cares in a special way for the people most forgotten.

Sure, it's not easy to remember and live each moment aware that nothing can snatch us from God's hands—even our worst failures and most serious sins. That's why a strong spiritual life is key. Take time each day to close your eyes and visualize yourself leaning back into God's arms like a little kid with a parent. Sit with that picture for several minutes. Ignore any thoughts about any tests, practices, or worries. Just rest in God's arms. Over time you'll notice that you worry less. You'll become more aware in your gut that, regardless of what happens, God will always be there to comfort, strengthen, and guide you.

So do your best. Develop your mind, body, and spirit. Reach for lofty goals. But always remember who embraces you every moment of every day.

Take :10 Reflect

If a word or phrase from the Gospel grabs your heart, sit quietly for several minutes, repeating it to yourself and asking God to show you how it applies to your life. Or, reflect and possibly journal on the following question:

- How would a deeper awareness that you live in God's hands change your worries?

Fifth Sunday of Easter
John 13:31–35

Love Your Friends Through Their Flaws

Take :05 Examine

How did I live out last week's Gospel message? What was tough? What was rewarding?

Take :05 Read

When Judas had left them, Jesus said, "Now is the Son of Man glorified, and God is glorified in him. If God is glorified in him, God will also glorify him in himself, and God will glorify him at once. My children, I will be with you only a little while longer. I give you a new commandment: love one another. As I have loved you, so you also should love one another. This is how all will know that you are my disciples, if you have love for one another."

I have a bad temper and a big mouth. And when they work together, it's not pretty. Unfortunately, that combination has caused me trouble and others pain through the years.

As I have worked on my relationship with Christ, my temper and mouth have caused fewer problems for everyone. But that's greatly due to friends in my religious order. My friends have challenged me—sometimes strongly—to be more patient and to watch my mouth. They've done that by pulling me aside in tense moments and by sitting me down after arguments. They've even done that by teasing me and making me laugh at myself. To sum it up, they've done that by loving me like Jesus loved his disciples.

That's Jesus' challenge to all Christians in this week's Gospel: Love one another as Jesus loved his first followers. Remember the Gospel stories. The Apostles weren't saints. The Gospel shows Jesus constantly correcting them. He catches them fighting with each other, ignoring hungry people who need their help, and sending sick people away who need healing. But through it all, he stands by them. He believes in their goodness and always tries to bring it out by helping them become better people. Why? Because he knew the world would be a better place if they continued to change and grow.

We can do the same thing for fellow Christians. We need to gently challenge one another to become better people while at the same time recognizing our own flaws. Real loyalty means pointing out a friend's mistakes and standing by that friend while he or she works to grow. People who feel accepted despite their flaws are more likely to change into happier and holier people. That's what has happened in my life.

And in the end, that's what the world needs—happier and holier Christians. So by loving fellow Christians the way Jesus loved his followers, you're changing the world.

Take :10 Reflect

If a word or phrase from the Gospel grabs your heart, sit quietly for several minutes, repeating it to yourself and asking God to show you how it applies to your life. Or, reflect and possibly journal on the following question:

• In what ways do you need to change so that your love for friends and family is more like Jesus' love for his followers?

Whose Peace—Jesus' or Rome's?

Take :05 Examine

How did I live out last week's Gospel message? What was tough? What was rewarding?

Take :05 Read

Jesus said to his disciples: "Whoever loves me will keep my word, and my Father will love him, and we will come to him and make our dwelling with him. Whoever does not love me does not keep my words; yet the word you hear is not mine but that of the Father who sent me.

"I have told you this while I am with you. The Advocate, the Holy Spirit, whom the Father will send in my name, will teach you everything and remind you of all that I told you. Peace I leave with you; my peace I give to you. Not as the world gives do I give it to you. Do not let your hearts be troubled or afraid. You heard me tell you, 'I am going away and I will come back to you.' If you loved me, you would rejoice that I am going to the Father; for the Father is greater than I. And now I have told you this before it happens, so that when it happens you may believe."

Peace.

As it was defined by Jesus of Nazareth, peace was a dangerous goal for the early Christians who lived in the Roman Empire.

The Roman Empire also brought "peace." But Roman leaders believed they could bring peace by conquering nations, crucifying rebels, and worshiping Roman gods. That means early Christians were radically different from their culture and their government. They followed a man who said peace comes from healing, forgiving, and serving others.

They chose to worship the God who stood for sacrifice and nonviolence instead of the Roman gods, who called for war and domination.

How about us today? Our nation resorts quickly to military solutions for global problems. Some U.S. leaders think all nations should bend to our national will. Many people seek peace by ignoring their conflicts with others or by shouting down people who disagree with them.

In contrast, I know some Catholic nuns who work full time to further Christ's peace. They organize nonviolent demonstrations against the use of military force to solve world problems. They teach people about Christian movements that have brought peace to war-torn areas through nonviolence. They train people to solve problems without violent words or actions. Like the early Christians, they look pretty radical to some. They are Christian heroes to me.

Easter is a good time to ask difficult questions about our notion of peace. Do we work for peace by forgiving others or by settling conflicts without violent words or actions? Do our national policies reflect Jesus' style of peacemaking or Rome's? Are we courageous enough to look as radical as our Christian ancestors?

Take :10 Reflect

If a word or phrase from the Gospel grabs your heart, sit quietly for several minutes, repeating it to yourself and asking God to show you how it applies to your life. Or, reflect and possibly journal on the following question:

- Where do you—or where does our country—need to change in order to more effectively stand for the peace Jesus offers the world?

Avoid Christian Cliques

Take :05 Examine

How did I live out last week's Gospel message? What was tough? What was rewarding?

Take :05 Read

Lifting up his eyes to heaven, Jesus prayed saying: "Holy Father, I pray not only for them, but also for those who will believe in me through their word, so that they may all be one, as you, Father, are in me and I in you, that they also may be in us, that the world may believe that you sent me. And I have given them the glory you gave me, so that they may be one, as we are one, I in them and you in me, that they may be brought to perfection as one, that the world may know that you sent me, and that you loved them even as you loved me. Father, they are your gift to me. I wish that where I am they also may be with me, that they may see my glory that you gave me, because you loved me before the foundation of the world. Righteous Father, the world also does not know you, but I know you, and they know that you sent me. I made known to them your name and I will make it known, that the love with which you loved me may be in them and I in them."

When I worked in a Catholic high school, our retreat program did a lot of good. It gave teens an opportunity to gather with peers and talk honestly about hope and fear, faith in and doubt about God. Teens almost always came away from the retreats feeling closer to God and to one another.

But sometimes all that good backfired. Occasionally, some teens that had not been on retreat came to me upset. They felt left out or ignored by their friends who went on retreat.

There's a real tension in Christian living that comes out in this week's Gospel. Jesus wants his followers to "be one." That means it's important for Christians to build strong relationships through things like retreats and youth groups. Those experiences help us love one another and God.

But Jesus says he wants us to be one so that the world knows about his message. That means the ultimate goal of all retreats and youth-group meetings is to spread Jesus' message to people who weren't there. So avoid forming retreat or youth-group cliques. It is important to live the values you learn on retreats and in youth groups. But do that without making people who weren't there feel like outsiders. Here's how.

Avoid making inside jokes from retreats or youth groups around people who weren't there. Go out of your way to invite new people to join your youth group, but don't pressure them or judge them if they refuse. Just live your Christian values around them. If you need to challenge them to change some behavior that could hurt themselves or others, do it with love and respect.

Maybe someday they'll ask why Jesus is so important to you.

Take :10 Reflect

If a word or phrase from the Gospel grabs your heart, sit quietly for several minutes, repeating it to yourself and asking God to show you how it applies to your life. Or, reflect and possibly journal on the following question:

- How can Christian teens avoid turning off other teens without sacrificing their Christian values?

The Holy Spirit 1: Fill Your Tank

Take :05 Examine

How did I live out last week's Gospel message? What was tough? What was rewarding?

Take :05 Read

On the evening of that first day of the week, when the doors were locked, where the disciples were, for fear of the Jews, Jesus came and stood in their midst and said to them, "Peace be with you." When he had said this, he showed them his hands and his side. The disciples rejoiced when they saw the Lord. Jesus said to them again, "Peace be with you. As the Father has sent me, so I send you." And when he had said this, he breathed on them and said to them, "Receive the Holy Spirit. Whose sins you forgive are forgiven them, and whose sins you retain are retained."

I have a couple friends with whom I don't like driving. Each likes to see how far *below* empty he can go with the fuel gauge before filling up. Both have run out of gas before. One even ran out on a back road in Central America!

I've known other people—teens and adults—who run out of gas in other ways. They start projects with a lot of energy and ideas but can't seem to finish them. That doesn't have to happen to us as Christians. Our fuel is the Holy Spirit. And the filling station is always open.

Some people have trouble understanding how the Holy Spirit can make a difference in daily life. I think this week's Gospel makes that clear. Jesus breathes on his Apostles and says, "Receive the Holy Spirit." He does that after saying that he sends us into the world as the Father sent him. So, Jesus gave us the Spirit as fuel for doing his mission.

What's the point? If you want to really see how the Spirit can impact your life, call on the Spirit's power to help you live like Jesus. You can do that in many ways. When you're ready to explode, stop and ask the Spirit to calm you. When you're ready to go along with the crowd instead of standing up for what's right, stop and ask the Spirit to boost you. When you feel like turning away from someone who needs you, stop and ask the Spirit to help you care.

This isn't magic. Like many things, you get better at letting the Spirit empower you the more often you call upon the Spirit. I know that I'm more able to feel the Spirit in clutch moments if I'm praying regularly each day. Again, like cars, we need regular maintenance (a daily prayer life), not just occasional trips to the gas station.

So fill up. There's a world full of people waiting for you to drive up with hope, healing, and justice.

Take :10 Reflect

If a word or phrase from the Gospel grabs your heart, sit quietly for several minutes, repeating it to yourself and asking God to show you how it applies to your life. Or, reflect and possibly journal on the following:

- Recall a time when a quick prayer in a difficult moment has helped you act more like Jesus.

The Holy Spirit 2: Get Out the Road Map

Take :05 Examine

How did I live out last week's Gospel message? What was tough? What was rewarding?

Take :05 Read

Jesus said to his disciples: "I have much more to tell you, but you cannot bear it now. But when he comes, the Spirit of truth, he will guide you to all truth. He will not speak on his own, but he will speak what he hears, and will declare to you the things that are coming. He will glorify me, because he will take from what is mine and declare it to you. Everything that the Father has is mine; for this reason I told you that he will take from what is mine and declare it to you."

(*Note:* This week's reflection connects with the one from last week.)

I hate driving with people who won't ask for directions or look at a road map. Aside from running out of gas, there's nothing I hate more than following a route on a hunch that it's the right way.

This brings us to the second way the Holy Spirit can make a huge difference in our lives. In this week's Gospel, Jesus promises his Apostles that "the Spirit of truth" will guide them. The same goes for us. The Spirit, in other words, is our road map.

Are you willing to follow it?

I've known a lot of teens who've struggled with questions like, Where should I go with my life? Isn't it nice to know there are directions?

God could've sent Jesus as a role model and then left the rest to us. But God knows us, loves us, and wants the best for us, so we have guidance whenever we want it. Here are some important tips to remember when you look for that guidance.

First, Jesus gave the Spirit to the Apostles as a group, not as individuals. So they found the Spirit's guidance by praying and talking together. Likewise, we need to connect with other Christians to find the Spirit's guidance. When you have a problem or need to make a decision pray and talk with other Christians. Talk with a priest or another spiritual guide when you need direction.

Second, the Spirit's guidance comes through the dead as well as the living. Our Christian community includes heroes who've gone before us, from the Apostles to modern-day folks like Mother Teresa. The Spirit guides us through their lives too. So read about them in the Bible, on the Internet, in religion books. Let their lives provide you with part of your road map.

Finding God's direction in your life isn't always easy. It can be confusing. You'll make wrong turns and hit some dead ends. I have. But every time I've reached for the Holy Spirit's help, I've found direction. And looking back I'm amazed at the journey.

It's been a great ride.

Take :10 Reflect

If a word or phrase from the Gospel grabs your heart, sit quietly for several minutes, repeating it to yourself and asking God to show you how it applies to your life. Or, reflect and possibly journal on the following:

- Recall a time when prayer or discussion with other Christians helped you find God's guidance.

It's Our Job Now to Feed the People

How did I live out last week's Gospel message? What was
tough? What was rewarding?

*Jesus spoke to the crowds about the kingdom of God, and he
healed those who needed to be cured. As the day was drawing
to a close, the Twelve approached him and said, "Dismiss the
crowd so that they can go to the surrounding villages and farms
and find lodging and provisions; for we are in a deserted place
here." He said to them, "Give them some food yourselves." They
replied, "Five loaves and two fish are all we have, unless we
ourselves go and buy food for all these people." Now the men
there numbered about five thousand. Then he said to his
disciples, "Have them sit down in groups of about fifty." They did
so and made them all sit down. Then taking the five loaves and
the two fish, and looking up to heaven, he said the blessing over
them, broke them, and gave them to the disciples to set before
the crowd. They all ate and were satisfied. And when the leftover
fragments were picked up, they filled twelve wicker baskets.*

I met an amazing young man one Christmas. Only thirteen
years old, he had organized a church blanket drive that had
collected dozens, maybe hundreds, of blankets for homeless
people. His mom told me that he first wanted to organize
the drive when he was seven, but that she told him to wait
until he was older.

This young man is the perfect example of someone who seems to have learned from this week's Gospel. In the Gospel story, the disciples face a hungry crowd and seem confused. They ask Jesus to do something. "Send them away," they say. But Jesus challenges them to do something. The result? The hungry people eat.

We have to remember that Jesus left our world, but Christ is still here. We are Christ's Body on earth. Each of us has a role to play in a world full of hunger and hopelessness. We all have the power to make a difference. But we need to work together and seek Jesus' guidance.

So don't just pray for Jesus to help others. He isn't coming back until the end. It's up to you and me to do the hard work of changing the world until then. Want world peace? Then pray for the ability to be a peacemaker. Want homes for the homeless? Then pray for the guidance to help homeless people in your town. Want healing in your family? Then pray for the strength to bring it yourself.

Jesus is still trying to feed hungry people. But we're his Body now. Let's get to work.

Take :10 Reflect

If a word or phrase from the Gospel grabs your heart, sit quietly for several minutes, repeating it to yourself and asking God to show you how it applies to your life. Or, reflect and possibly journal on the following question:

- Who inspires you to believe you can help work Christ's miracles in today's world?

Healthy Humility Heals

Take :05 Examine

How did I live out last week's Gospel message? What was tough? What was rewarding?

Take :05 Read

When Jesus had finished all his words to the people, he entered Capernaum. A centurion there had a slave who was ill and about to die, and he was valuable to him. When he heard about Jesus, he sent elders of the Jews to him, asking him to come and save the life of his slave. They approached Jesus and strongly urged him to come, saying, "He deserves to have you do this for him, for he loves our nation and built the synagogue for us." And Jesus went with them, but when he was only a short distance from the house, the centurion sent friends to tell him, "Lord, do not trouble yourself, for I am not worthy to have you enter under my roof. Therefore, I did not consider myself worthy to come to you; but say the word and let my servant be healed. For I too am a person subject to authority, with soldiers subject to me. And I say to one, 'Go,' and he goes; and to another, 'Come here,' and he comes; and to my slave, 'Do this,' and he does it." When Jesus heard this he was amazed at him and, turning, said to the crowd following him, "I tell you, not even in Israel have I found such faith." When the messengers returned to the house, they found the slave in good health.

I read recently about a star college basketball player who was ordained as a Christian minister. The article said his relationship with God was more important to him than his basketball career.

Wow! There's a guy who hasn't let his power blind him.

We meet another guy like that in this week's Gospel. The Roman centurion had authority. He commanded soldiers. He was popular with the townspeople because he helped them build a synagogue.

But he recognized real power and authority when he heard about Jesus. Then he humbly asked for help.

It's easy to be cocky when you have talent or power. If you're smart or in a position of authority, you might think you know it all. If you're strong, you might think you can do it all. This week's Gospel passage reminds us to remember our limits. Pride can be our downfall.

Do we go it alone when we face problems? Are we afraid that asking for help shows weakness? Like the centurion, we need to regularly approach Jesus humbly, conscious of our limits and where we need help. We need to remind ourselves that we don't have all the answers. God—through our prayer, through our reading of the Scriptures, and through other Christians—has help waiting for us.

We echo this Gospel passage each Mass when we say, "Lord, I am not worthy to receive you, but only say the word and I shall be healed." That means we're limited, not bad. And it's okay to be limited, because our God is constantly seeking ways to heal and strengthen us.

Take :10 Reflect

If a word or phrase from the Gospel grabs your heart, sit quietly for several minutes, repeating it to yourself and asking God to show you how it applies to your life. Or, reflect and possibly journal on the following question:

- Has pride or success ever caused you to ignore God or think you don't need God's help?

Be On the Lookout

Take :05 Examine

How did I live out last week's Gospel message? What was tough? What was rewarding?

Take :05 Read

Jesus journeyed to a city called Nain, and his disciples and a large crowd accompanied him. As he drew near to the gate of the city, a man who had died was being carried out, the only son of his mother, and she was a widow. A large crowd from the city was with her. When the Lord saw her, he was moved with pity for her and said to her, "Do not weep." He stepped forward and touched the coffin; at this the bearers halted, and he said, "Young man, I tell you, arise!" The dead man sat up and began to speak, and Jesus gave him to his mother. Fear seized them all, and they glorified God, exclaiming, "A great prophet has arisen in our midst," and "God has visited his people." This report about him spread through the whole of Judea and in all the surrounding region.

It's one thing to help people when they ask. It's another to notice that people need help even though they aren't asking for it.

I'm a busy guy. My days are usually pretty packed. I'm good at helping people, if it's on my calendar. Unfortunately, I think I miss people who need help—but don't ask for it—when I rush through a day, moving from task to task. Like Jesus, I need to be on the lookout for people who need me.

Look at Jesus in this week's Gospel. The widow didn't approach him; Jesus approached her when he saw her weeping. The story shows how focused Jesus was on looking for people who needed him; he wasn't focused just on his daily tasks.

And the widow desperately needed his help. In many ancient cultures, it was very difficult for unmarried women and widows to support themselves. Women without husbands or sons were destined for extreme poverty. The widow in this story lost not only her son but everything. Jesus knew that. He went to her so God's healing power could restore her son's life and her hope.

How about us? How often do people pass us who feel like they've lost everything? Classmates who've broken up with a girl or boyfriend. Parents struggling at work. Homeless people looking for shelter or a hot meal. Do we keep our eyes open for them? Do we ask God for the vision to see them and the grace to help them? Or do we rush through the day focused on what's next in *our* world?

Christians are called to be on the lookout for people who suffer. Ask God to focus your vision beyond your schedule. Look for the widows that come across your path. Reach out. Your compassion will cause people in this day and age to echo the people in this week's Gospel who watched Jesus and said, "God has visited his people."

Take :10 Reflect

If a word or phrase from the Gospel grabs your heart, sit quietly for several minutes, repeating it to yourself and asking God to show you how it applies to your life. Or, reflect and possibly journal on the following question:

- Who is one person in your life who inspires you by his or her willingness to drop everything to help someone, even if that someone may not be asking for help?

Find Some "Sinners" and Learn

Take :05 Examine

How did I live out last week's Gospel message? What was tough? What was rewarding?

Take :05 Read

A Pharisee invited Jesus to dine with him, and he entered the Pharisee's house and reclined at table. Now there was a sinful woman in the city who learned that he was at table in the house of the Pharisee. Bringing an alabaster flask of ointment, she stood behind him at his feet weeping and began to bathe his feet with her tears. Then she wiped them with her hair, kissed them, and anointed them with the ointment. When the Pharisee who had invited him saw this he said to himself, "If this man were a prophet, he would know who and what sort of woman this is who is touching him, that she is a sinner." Jesus said to him in reply, "Simon, I have something to say to you." "Tell me, teacher," he said. "Two people were in debt to a certain creditor; one owed five hundred days' wages and the other owed fifty. Since they were unable to repay the debt, he forgave it for both. Which of them will love him more?" Simon said in reply, "The one, I suppose, whose larger debt was forgiven." He said to him, "You have judged rightly."

Then he turned to the woman and said to Simon, "Do you see this woman? When I entered your house, you did not give me water for my feet, but she has bathed them with her tears and wiped them with her hair. You did not give me a kiss, but she has not ceased kissing my feet since the time I entered. You did not anoint my head with oil, but she anointed my feet with oint-

ment. So I tell you, her many sins have been forgiven because she has shown great love." (Luke 7:36–47)

"How are you today?" I asked the guy in line at the soup kitchen. "God has blessed me," he answered with a smile.

Sometimes people our society looks down on the most—like homeless people—show us the deepest faith. That's what happens in this week's Gospel. A sinner shows her gratitude to Jesus. His praise for her actions and his forgiveness of her sins must have brought her great comfort. She probably needed it. As a sinner in Jesus' time, she would have been shunned by many people.

Maybe she had been waiting years for Jesus' message about a God who welcomes all people, forgives all people, and heals all people. Maybe Simon doesn't show Jesus the same love because he can't face his own sins and need for God.

I've learned a lot in my life from people others look down on. In them I've often seen the courage to admit weakness and need for God. When I've followed their example, God has seemed much closer to me. And when I've called out for help, it has come, often causing me to drop to my knees in thanksgiving, just like the woman in this Gospel.

Take :10 Reflect

If a word or phrase from the Gospel grabs your heart, sit quietly for several minutes, repeating it to yourself and asking God to show you how it applies to your life. Or, reflect and possibly journal on the following question:

- Why is it difficult for you to admit your sins or weaknesses to God or to other Christians?

Who Do You Say He Is?

Take :05 Examine

How did I live out last week's Gospel message? What was tough? What was rewarding?

Take :05 Read

Once when Jesus was praying in solitude, and the disciples were with him, he asked them, "Who do the crowds say that I am?" They said in reply, "John the Baptist; others, Elijah; still others, 'One of the ancient prophets has arisen.'" Then he said to them, "But who do you say that I am?" Peter said in reply, "The Christ of God." He rebuked them and directed them not to tell this to anyone.

He said, "The Son of Man must suffer greatly and be rejected by the elders, the chief priests, and the scribes, and be killed and on the third day be raised." Then he said to all, "If anyone wishes to come after me, he must deny himself and take up his cross daily and follow me. For whoever wishes to save his life will lose it, but whoever loses his life for my sake will save it."

Many years ago an NBA player angrily announced that basketball players aren't paid to be role models, so young people should stop looking at them that way. The statement came because some parents were criticizing basketball players for acting immorally off the court.

That player was right. Don't make an athlete your role model for life. Life is more than sports. But don't let Jesus be *just* a role model either.

What?

Yep, I said it. Don't make Jesus *just* a role model. Role models set examples to follow. But they don't necessarily help you follow those examples. That depends on your ability.

Jesus is more than a role model. Jesus is God. There's a big difference. We want to follow Jesus' example for living, but we can't do it on our own. That's what makes Jesus more than a role model. Because he is God, Jesus can send the world his Spirit. And we can follow his example only with the Spirit's strength and guidance. Without the Spirit's strength and guidance, we're doomed to fail.

A lot of people give up on Christian living because they think it's just too hard. Or they argue that Jesus' message about forgiveness and peace is unrealistic. That might be because they see Jesus as *just* a role model—one of many lifestyle options. Maybe they don't realize Jesus doesn't expect us to follow his example using our strength. Maybe they don't realize that Jesus' lifestyle seems more and more realistic the more you let the Spirit shape your vision and strengthen you through prayer.

So who do you say he is? Let him be more than your role model. Let Jesus be your God, your source of all life, strength, goodness, and hope. Let him help with every decision. Let him show you the way to go and help you get there. Let him inspire you, forgive you, heal you, and strengthen you. You can use his strength and vision every moment of every day. Ordinary role models can't give you that!

Take :10 Reflect

If a word or phrase from the Gospel grabs your heart, sit quietly for several minutes, repeating it to yourself and asking God to show you how it applies to your life. Or, reflect and possibly journal on the following question:

- Where in your life do you need Jesus' strength most to live as a Christian?

Are You Looking Backward or Plowing Forward?

Take :05 Examine

How did I live out last week's Gospel message? What was tough? What was rewarding?

Take :05 Read

When the days for Jesus' being taken up were fulfilled, he resolutely determined to journey to Jerusalem, and he sent messengers ahead of him. On the way they entered a Samaritan village to prepare for his reception there, but they would not welcome him because the destination of his journey was Jerusalem. When the disciples James and John saw this they asked, "Lord, do you want us to call down fire from heaven to consume them?" Jesus turned and rebuked them, and they journeyed to another village.

As they were proceeding on their journey someone said to him, "I will follow you wherever you go." Jesus answered him, "Foxes have dens and birds of the sky have nests, but the Son of Man has nowhere to rest his head."

And to another he said, "Follow me." But he replied, "Lord, let me go first and bury my father." But he answered him, "Let the dead bury their dead. But you, go and proclaim the kingdom of God." And another said, "I will follow you, Lord, but first let me say farewell to my family at home." To him Jesus said, "No one who sets a hand to the plow and looks to what was left behind is fit for the kingdom of God."

I live in Illinois. Each summer I pass rows and rows of corn when I'm driving. As the season progresses, I watch spring's green sprouts turn into summer's tall stalks. It's a miracle. But it also depends on farmers who know how to plow.

In this week's Gospel, Jesus compares discipleship to plowing. Christians are like farmers. They bring new life into the world because they plow forward with their faith—something you can't do if you're always looking back to the past.

Should you ignore your past? No.

I have a friend who made a lot of mistakes in life. He wanted to become more Christian but found it difficult. Why? He never learned from his mistakes or apologized to the people he hurt. As a result, he could never plow forward. By ignoring his past, he actually became stuck in it.

Following Christ doesn't mean forgetting past mistakes and moving ahead. That doesn't work. You can't move forward in life with Jesus until you learn from mistakes and reconcile broken relationships.

Deal with your past mistakes and sins. It will help you set a hand to the plow, move forward, and bring new life into the world.

Take :10 Reflect

If a word or phrase from the Gospel grabs your heart, sit quietly for several minutes, repeating it to yourself and asking God to show you how it applies to your life. Or, reflect and possibly journal on the following questions:

- What past sins or broken relationships hold you back? How has your past made you a better disciple?

He's Appointed You Too

Take :05 Examine

How did I live out last week's Gospel message? What was tough? What was rewarding?

Take :05 Read

At that time the Lord appointed seventy-two others whom he sent ahead of him in pairs to every town and place he intended to visit. He said to them, "The harvest is abundant but the laborers are few; so ask the master of the harvest to send out laborers for his harvest. Go on your way; behold, I am sending you like lambs among wolves. Carry no money bag, no sack, no sandals; and greet no one along the way. Into whatever house you enter, first say, 'Peace to this household.' If a peaceful person lives there, your peace will rest on him; but if not, it will return to you. Stay in the same house and eat and drink what is offered to you, for the laborer deserves his payment. Do not move about from one house to another. Whatever town you enter and they welcome you, eat what is set before you, cure the sick in it and say to them, 'The kingdom of God is at hand for you.' Whatever town you enter and they do not receive you, go out into the streets and say, 'The dust of your town that clings to our feet, even that we shake off against you.' Yet know this: the kingdom of God is at hand." (Luke 10:1–11)

Their faces lit up. They hadn't realized the difference they would make. After all, they were just four teens.

They believed in peace. So they decided to start a youth retreat to teach how Christians can fight racial prejudice.

The four teens glowed with confidence after the leaders they helped choose for the retreat ended a day of training. They looked on as their Hispanic, Anglo, and African American teen leaders shook hands and committed to join them in their peace project.

"The Lord appointed seventy-two others" to "cure the sick" and announce that "the kingdom of God is at hand."

This Gospel tells a story that's two thousand years old but also brand new. These four peace-building teens heard Jesus' instructions as clearly as the first disciples. Like them, they went forward on faith. They didn't know if other teens would welcome their ideas or ridicule them. Like the first disciples, the four teens also cured sickness by helping other teens take a stand against prejudice. And like the first disciples, they were amazed at the power Jesus gave them.

Did you know Jesus has appointed you too? Many teens doubt themselves. Some look in the mirror and think they can't make a difference. I think those first disciples thought the same thing. Remember, they were ordinary people. Most were probably poor and uneducated. They probably felt powerless too, until Jesus came into their lives.

Then they changed the world. But the job's not done. Just look around your school, and you'll see plenty of sickness. Will *you* go when he sends you?

Take :10 Reflect

If a word or phrase from the Gospel grabs your heart, sit quietly for several minutes, repeating it to yourself and asking God to show you how it applies to your life. Or, reflect and possibly journal on the following question:

- What sickness in the world should you, or do you, help cure?

A Story That Needs Retelling

Take :05 Examine

How did I live out last week's Gospel message? What was tough? What was rewarding?

Take :05 Read

There was a scholar of the law who stood up to test him and said, "Teacher, what must I do to inherit eternal life?" Jesus said to him, "What is written in the law? How do you read it?" He said in reply,

"You shall love the Lord, your God,
with all your heart,
with all your being,
with all your strength,
and with all your mind,
and your neighbor as yourself."

He replied to him, "You have answered correctly; do this and you will live."

But because he wished to justify himself, he said to Jesus, "And who is my neighbor?" Jesus replied, "A man fell victim to robbers as he went down from Jerusalem to Jericho. They stripped and beat him and went off leaving him half-dead. A priest happened to be going down that road, but when he saw him, he passed by on the opposite side. Likewise a Levite came to the place, and when he saw him, he passed by on the opposite side. But a Samaritan traveler who came upon him was moved with compassion at the sight. He approached the victim, poured oil and wine over his wounds and bandaged them. Then he lifted him up on his own animal, took him to an inn, and cared for him. The next day he took out two silver coins and gave them to the innkeeper with the instruction, 'Take care of him. If you spend more than what I have given you, I shall repay you on my way back.' Which of these three, in your opinion, was neighbor to the robbers' victim?" He answered, "The one who treated him with mercy." Jesus said to him, "Go and do likewise."

Just days after 9-11, an angry mob gathered blocks from a Chicago area mosque. The mob marched toward the mosque to seek revenge for the 9-11 attacks. Mob members apparently reasoned that all Muslims are terrorists because a few Muslims used their faith to justify mass murder.

Religious bigotry, which caused so much hatred in Jesus' time, is alive and well. What did Jesus say about it? This week's Gospel tells it all.

Many Jews in Jesus' time shunned Samaritans because they were the descendants of Jews who had married people from different ethnic and religious backgrounds. So Jesus must have shaken this scholar of the Law and his prejudices when he made the Samaritan the good guy in this story.

The mosque I mentioned found protection that night, and later many local Christians spoke out against the religious bigotry that spurred the march. Thus, they retold the story of the Good Samaritan in their own words. Is that a story you're willing to share?

Take :10 Reflect

If a word or phrase from the Gospel grabs your heart, sit quietly for several minutes, repeating it to yourself and asking God to show you how it applies to your life. Or, reflect and possibly journal on the following question:

• Where have you witnessed religious or ethnic prejudice?

Mary Learned from Jesus—Can We?

Take :05 Examine

How did I live out last week's Gospel message? What was tough? What was rewarding?

Take :05 Read

Jesus entered a village where a woman whose name was Martha welcomed him. She had a sister named Mary who sat beside the Lord at his feet listening to him speak. Martha, burdened with much serving, came to him and said, "Lord, do you not care that my sister has left me by myself to do the serving? Tell her to help me." The Lord said to her in reply, "Martha, Martha, you are anxious and worried about many things. There is need of only one thing. Mary has chosen the better part and it will not be taken from her."

There are many young women in this nation who see themselves as ministers because of my friend Karen.

I worked with Karen as a campus minister for four years. She worked hard for all students. But she particularly took pride in helping young women develop confidence as leaders.

Jesus also valued women disciples highly. And this Gospel shows it. In Jesus' time women were little more than property. They had few rights. They certainly weren't allowed to study at the feet of religious teachers. But Jesus saw things differently. He encouraged women to learn from him and follow him. He appeared to a woman first after his Resurrection. He defied the stereotypes and sexism of his day.

Many women tell me they think our society still suffers from warped views about a woman's role. Ads seem to argue that women have no value unless they wear the latest fashions. Teachers have said that some teen girls don't offer answers in class out of fear that boys don't find smart girls attractive. Women are underrepresented in leadership in many parts of society. A frighteningly high number of women suffer abuse each year by men who think women have no right to refuse their physical advances.

My friend is a good example of someone who learned from Jesus about a woman's role. All Christians need to look critically at negative stereotypes of women in our culture and stand up to anything that denies women equal rights in politics, business, or religion.

Mary sat at Jesus' feet to learn. Maybe we should do the same thing if we wonder about a woman's "role."

Take :10 Reflect

If a word or phrase from the Gospel grabs your heart, sit quietly for several minutes, repeating it to yourself and asking God to show you how it applies to your life. Or, reflect and possibly journal on the following:

- Identify any stereotypes or policies in our society that you think are contrary to Jesus' view of women.

You'll Get What You Need

Take :05 Examine

How did I live out last week's Gospel message? What was tough? What was rewarding?

Take :05 Read

And [Jesus] said to them, "Suppose one of you has a friend to whom he goes at midnight and says, 'Friend, lend me three loaves of bread, for a friend of mine has arrived at my house from a journey and I have nothing to offer him,' and he says in reply from within, 'Do not bother me; the door has already been locked and my children and I are already in bed. I cannot get up to give you anything.' I tell you, if he does not get up to give the visitor the loaves because of their friendship, he will get up to give him whatever he needs because of his persistence.

"And I tell you, ask and you will receive; seek and you will find; knock and the door will be opened to you. For everyone who asks, receives; and the one who seeks, finds; and to the one who knocks, the door will be opened. What father among you would hand his son a snake when he asks for a fish? Or hand him a scorpion when he asks for an egg? If you then, who are wicked, know how to give good gifts to your children, how much more will the Father in heaven give the Holy Spirit to those who ask him?" (Luke 11:5–13)

A few years ago, the faculty at my high school gathered to pray for the recovery of a teacher with cancer. He recovered dramatically. About a year later, the faculty gathered again to pray for another teacher fighting cancer. She died from the disease within the year.

So why did God answer one prayer and not the other? Or, if God answered both prayers, why the different outcomes?

This week's Gospel will help you understand. Jesus says God doesn't always answer our prayers by giving us what we want. First, Jesus compares God to a person who gives his friend what he needs. Then he says God will answer our prayers by giving us the Holy Spirit.

What do you expect from prayer? Most of us pray for things we want, but God often gives us something we need—the courage and commitment to do God's will in tough times. You might want a good grade, but what you need are better study habits. So the answer to your prayer might be a teacher challenging you to work harder. You might pray for God to spare a loved one from an illness. God might answer by strengthening you with the Spirit so you can comfort your sick loved one. You might want a better life for the poor. And God might answer your prayer by calling your attention to an opportunity to serve poor people in your community.

Sure, our prayers might work miracles for others. But more often our prayers work miracles in us. Here's a challenge: Keep track of your prayers in a journal, and also keep track of possible changes you see in yourself or your life. Talk with a minister about your search for answers to prayer. See if God makes changes in the world or in you.

Take :10 Reflect

If a word or phrase from the Gospel grabs your heart, sit quietly for several minutes, repeating it to yourself and asking God to show you how it applies to your life. Or, reflect and possibly journal on the following question:

- Can you remember a time you were inspired to help someone after praying for him or her?

Too Many Toys, Not Enough Fun?

Take :05 Examine

How did I live out last week's Gospel message? What was tough? What was rewarding?

Take :05 Read

Someone in the crowd said to Jesus, "Teacher, tell my brother to share the inheritance with me." He replied to him, "Friend, who appointed me as your judge and arbitrator?" Then he said to the crowd, "Take care to guard against all greed, for though one may be rich, one's life does not consist of possessions."

Then he told them a parable. "There was a rich man whose land produced a bountiful harvest. He asked himself, 'What shall I do, for I do not have space to store my harvest?' And he said, 'This is what I shall do: I shall tear down my barns and build larger ones. There I shall store all my grain and other goods and I shall say to myself, "Now as for you, you have so many good things stored up for many years, rest, eat, drink, be merry!"' But God said to him, 'You fool, this night your life will be demanded of you; and the things you have prepared, to whom will they belong?' Thus will it be for all who store up treasure for themselves but are not rich in what matters to God."

One night I was volunteering at a shelter when I found dozens of hot dogs in the fridge. Knowing the homeless guests were hungry, I handed out all the hot dogs.

Another guest, James, arrived a little later. Smiling, he asked me to heat up a few of his hot dogs. Embarrassed, I realized that the hot dogs I had given out were James's hot dogs. I quickly apologized and offered to replace them. He laughed at my mistake and said, "Don't worry about it. As long as all the people ate, that's all I care about."

James was the exact opposite of the man in Jesus' parable this week.

This Gospel is important for Americans. Our culture pushes us to buy nonstop and do whatever we can to get more money and more things for ourselves. Some people joke that those who die with the most toys win. That's an easy trap to fall into, but Winston Churchill once said something like "you make a living with what you get, but you make a life with what you give."

A "more for me" attitude can take over your life and kill relationships. This week's Gospel condemns greed not because greedy people go to hell but because greedy people construct their own hell on earth.

Greed traps people in hell by keeping them from the best part of life, that which matters to God—sacrifice for others; service to the poor; relationships based on character, not appearance. You build a life—and find real happiness—by using your talents for others and putting their needs first.

I still forget that sometimes. That's why I'm grateful God sends people like James to remind me.

Take :10 Reflect

If a word or phrase from the Gospel grabs your heart, sit quietly for several minutes, repeating it to yourself and asking God to show you how it applies to your life. Or, reflect and possibly journal on the following questions:

- When have you seen greed hurt people? Has it ever hurt you?

The End Is Near?

Take :05 Examine

How did I live out last week's Gospel message? What was tough? What was rewarding?

Take :05 Read

Jesus said to his disciples: "Gird your loins and light your lamps and be like servants who await their master's return from a wedding, ready to open immediately when he comes and knocks. Blessed are those servants whom the master finds vigilant on his arrival. Amen, I say to you, he will gird himself, have the servants recline at table, and proceed to wait on them. And should he come in the second or third watch and find them prepared in this way, blessed are those servants. Be sure of this: if the master of the house had known the hour when the thief was coming, he would not have let his house be broken into. You also must be prepared, for at an hour you do not expect, the Son of Man will come." (Luke 12:35–40)

I was saddened a few years ago when a teen came to me upset. He was trying to live a Christian life, but he kept falling short. That worried him because some Christians had convinced him the world was ending soon. "I'm worried that Jesus won't take me with him," he said.

There's a lot of talk out there about the world's end. Some Christian books predict exactly how and when it will happen. Some people even use fear about the world's end and God's judgment to motivate people to follow Jesus.

Luke wrote this week's Gospel for early Christians who expected Jesus to return fairly soon. He urges Christians to be prepared, but he is also skeptical of people who claim to know when or how he's coming.

That's good advice for us. We don't know how the world will end. People who claim to find details about it in the Scriptures usually are misreading the Bible. We need to steer clear of people who use fear tactics to spread the Gospel. Our God motivates through love, not fear, always reminding us that we're loved despite our sins. So don't worry about whether the world might end before you're "good enough" in God's eyes.

It's our job to wait, not worry. We wait by praying and worshiping. We wait by doing our best and acknowledging our sins. We wait by serving the poor. We wait by opening up to Christians we trust. When you wait in these ways, you'll be surprised. Suddenly you'll realize God's grace and peace is with you—and the Master has arrived.

Take :10 Reflect

If a word or phrase from the Gospel grabs your heart, sit quietly for several minutes, repeating it to yourself and asking God to show you how it applies to your life. Or, reflect and possibly journal on the following question:

• Can you remember a time when you were suddenly surprised because you felt like God was with you?

Prince of Peace?

Take :05 Examine

How did I live out last week's Gospel message? What was tough? What was rewarding?

Take :05 Read

Jesus said to his disciples: "I have come to set the earth on fire, and how I wish it were already blazing! There is a baptism with which I must be baptized, and how great is my anguish until it is accomplished! Do you think that I have come to establish peace on the earth? No, I tell you, but rather division. From now on a household of five will be divided, three against two and two against three; a father will be divided against his son and a son against his father, a mother against her daughter and a daughter against her mother, a mother-in-law against her daughter-in-law and a daughter-in-law against her mother-in-law."

Wow. Some Prince of Peace this guy was. Splitting up families, causing division. You sure you want in on this?

Jesus almost sounds sad in this Gospel passage. Maybe this story recalls one of the first times he realized people wouldn't accept his Good News. Maybe that reality crushed him.

I've seen that happen to a lot of teens after youth-group meetings, retreats, or service trips. They feel filled with Good News but run into friends and family members who call them unrealistic, naïve, or Bible-thumpers. I've also seen conflict sparked when Christian teens stand up for what's right, in front of friends or classmates.

Yeah, Jesus was right. Conflict is definitely part of the package. The peace Jesus brings isn't a calm in which no one gets angry. Jesus makes it clear he stands for the peace that can come only when all people find respect and justice. But the people who call others to respect all people and to live justly—hopefully, you and me—quite often spark conflict.

So the real question is, How will you deal with conflict as a Christian?

Here are some tips from a guy who has faced it, made some mistakes, and learned from them. First, don't back down from it. Conflict can strengthen relationships if you deal with it nonviolently. Every time you stand up nonviolently for your beliefs despite conflict, your self-esteem grows. Second, remember that our God is nonviolent. Resolve conflict without name-calling, yelling, or becoming physically violent. That can be hard. But the more you practice, the better you get. Third, you're not alone. Pray for strength to remain faithful, even during conflict, and reach out to other Christians—especially adult ministers—for support and advice when times get tough.

So, yeah, conflict is part of the deal for Christians. And it can get ugly. But the Lord has been through it and won't leave you in the lurch.

Take :10 Reflect

If a word or phrase from the Gospel grabs your heart, sit quietly for several minutes, repeating it to yourself and asking God to show you how it applies to your life. Or, reflect and possibly journal on the following question:

- When have you seen Christian living spark conflict with friends or family?

Remember Your Dinner Partner

Take :05 Examine

How did I live out last week's Gospel message? What was tough? What was rewarding?

Take :05 Read

Jesus passed through towns and villages, teaching as he went and making his way to Jerusalem. Someone asked him, "Lord, will only a few people be saved?" He answered them, "Strive to enter through the narrow gate, for many, I tell you, will attempt to enter but will not be strong enough. After the master of the house has arisen and locked the door, then will you stand outside knocking and saying, 'Lord, open the door for us.' He will say to you in reply, 'I do not know where you are from.' And you will say, 'We ate and drank in your company and you taught in our streets.' Then he will say to you, 'I do not know where you are from. Depart from me, all you evildoers!' And there will be wailing and grinding of teeth when you see Abraham, Isaac, and Jacob and all the prophets in the kingdom of God and you yourselves cast out. And people will come from the east and the west and from the north and the south and will recline at table in the kingdom of God. For behold, some are last who will be first, and some are first who will be last."

Was Jesus talking about the church parking lot in this Gospel?

Watch a church parking lot after Mass. See who lets others go first and who races to be the first out, cutting off other parishioners.

Or maybe Jesus was talking about the sign of peace. I remember one parishioner who refused to offer it to another because he was angry with him.

Or maybe Jesus was talking about who is welcome at church. I remember a parishioner who was angry when her church let homeless people spend the night in a parish building.

I think Jesus was talking about all of the above in this week's Gospel. You see, going to church, where we eat and drink in Jesus' company, is really pretty easy. It takes about an hour. But after the final blessing, some people think they've done their part for the week and don't connect that "meal" with their behavior for the next six days.

But following Jesus requires much more. The challenge we face is letting the Sunday Eucharist shape our lives all week long. How does your weekly meal with Jesus shape how you play sports, treat outsiders, live with family, work at your job, and act at school?

And there's another challenge in this reading. We might be surprised, Jesus says, by who we meet at God's banquet in heaven. I've met homeless people who never go to church but are more compassionate than some people I know who go to church daily.

So go to church. Eat and drink in Jesus' company. But remember your dinner partner for the rest of the week. And also remember he dines with a lot of people we'll never see in church.

Take :10 Reflect

If a word or phrase from the Gospel grabs your heart, sit quietly for several minutes, repeating it to yourself and asking God to show you how it applies to your life. Or, reflect and possibly journal on the following question:

- If you were on trial for being a Christian, would the prosecution find enough evidence if they looked only at the way you live your life Monday through Saturday?

Who's at Your Lunch Table?

Take :05 Examine

How did I live out last week's Gospel message? What was
tough? What was rewarding?

Take :05 Read

*On a sabbath Jesus went to dine at the home of one of the
leading Pharisees, and the people there were observing him
carefully.*

*He told a parable to those who had been invited, noticing
how they were choosing the places of honor at the table. "When
you are invited by someone to a wedding banquet, do not recline
at table in the place of honor. A more distinguished guest than
you may have been invited by him, and the host who invited both
of you may approach you and say, 'Give your place to this man,'
and then you would proceed with embarrassment to take the
lowest place. Rather, when you are invited, go and take the
lowest place so that when the host comes to you he may say,
'My friend, move up to a higher position.' Then you will enjoy the
esteem of your companions at the table. For everyone who exalts himself will be humbled, but the one who humbles himself
will be exalted." Then he said to the host who invited him,
"When you hold a lunch or a dinner, do not invite your friends or
your brothers or your relatives or your wealthy neighbors, in case
they may invite you back and you have repayment. Rather, when
you hold a banquet, invite the poor, the crippled, the lame, the
blind; blessed indeed will you be because of their inability to
repay you. For you will be repaid at the resurrection of the
righteous."*

The school cafeteria. Over there are the jocks. There's the drama club. There's the band. There's that one kid who always eats alone. Who will you eat with? Who wouldn't you be caught dead eating with? Those are the questions Jesus asks in this week's Gospel.

Parties and meals are social time. It's pretty normal to spend that time with friends and people who share your interests. But sometimes friendships can become cliques that exclude or look down on others.

Jesus calls us to expand our circles of friends. Why? Because many people need our company. Meals were huge in Jesus' ministry. He brought outcasts to meals with people of honor. He ate in the homes of people considered sinners. His meals revealed God's Reign—where everyone has a place around the table.

He tells his followers to stop worrying about whether their seat location proves they're honorable. He asks them to welcome outcasts to their meals and into their lives.

What does that mean for us? Reach out. Each cafeteria has teens that sit alone. Invite them to your table. Each school has teens that are friendless. Welcome them into your circle of friends. Each city has nursing homes with lonely people. Find yourself another grandpa or grandma.

Honor the people others forget, and others will see that Jesus' ministry continues.

Take :10 Reflect

If a word or phrase from the Gospel grabs your heart, sit quietly for several minutes, repeating it to yourself and asking God to show you how it applies to your life. Or, reflect and possibly journal on the following question:

- What concrete step could you take to follow this Gospel next week?

Did He Say *Hate?*

Take :05 Examine

How did I live out last week's Gospel message? What was tough? What was rewarding?

Take :05 Read

Great crowds were traveling with Jesus, and he turned and addressed them, "If anyone comes to me without hating his father and mother, wife and children, brothers and sisters, and even his own life, he cannot be my disciple. Whoever does not carry his own cross and come after me cannot be my disciple. Which of you wishing to construct a tower does not first sit down and calculate the cost to see if there is enough for its completion? Otherwise, after laying the foundation and finding himself unable to finish the work the onlookers should laugh at him and say, 'This one began to build but did not have the resources to finish.' Or what king marching into battle would not first sit down and decide whether with ten thousand troops he can successfully oppose another king advancing upon him with twenty thousand troops? But if not, while he is still far away, he will send a delegation to ask for peace terms. In the same way, anyone of you who does not renounce all his possessions cannot be my disciple."

I had an interesting meeting with a mom when I was a parish youth minister. The woman's daughter had spent a lot of time with me at youth-group activities. So Mom wanted to make sure I was an okay guy.

I tell that story because this Gospel highlights this fact for many teens: Active discipleship can raise questions at home. Some parents get concerned when their teen starts making friends Mom and Dad don't know. Bad church ex-peri-ences can make it hard for some parents to accept a teen's good experiences. Parents who want more family time can get frustrat-ed when a teen wants to spend more time at church activities.

So your commitment to Jesus might cause friction at home, but don't misunderstand the Gospel. Jesus says to "hate" people, but according to Scripture scholars, he doesn't mean we should feel hatred. He means we should choose God's will over all people and things. And that should make us treat family and friends with more love.

If your faith choices do cause friction at home, here are some tips for responding with love:

- **Talk and listen.** Many parents just want to know what you're up to. Make time to discuss your faith choices with them.

- **Be patient.** Many parents struggle with faith. That can make it hard for them to understand yours.

- **Value family time.** Don't forget that discipleship calls us to serve our families, not just our parishes, youth groups, and the poor.

- **Seek help.** If tension is high at home, find an adult minister who can help you choose a Christian response.

- **Give them a break.** It's tough raising a teen—even a Christian one.

Take :10 Reflect

If a word or phrase from the Gospel grabs your heart, sit quietly for several minutes, repeating it to yourself and asking God to show you how it applies to your life. Or, reflect and possibly journal on the following question:

- When has a faith choice caused friction between you and your parents or friends?

God Never Gives Up on You

Take :05 Examine

How did I live out last week's Gospel message? What was tough? What was rewarding?

Take :05 Read

Tax collectors and sinners were all drawing near to listen to Jesus, but the Pharisees and scribes began to complain, saying, "This man welcomes sinners and eats with them." So to them he addressed this parable. "What man among you having a hundred sheep and losing one of them would not leave the ninety-nine in the desert and go after the lost one until he finds it? And when he does find it, he sets it on his shoulders with great joy and, upon his arrival home, he calls together his friends and neighbors and says to them, 'Rejoice with me because I have found my lost sheep.' I tell you, in just the same way there will be more joy in heaven over one sinner who repents than over ninety-nine righteous people who have no need of repentance.

"Or what woman having ten coins and losing one would not light a lamp and sweep the house, searching carefully until she finds it? And when she does find it, she calls together her friends and neighbors and says to them, 'Rejoice with me because I have found the coin that I lost.' In just the same way, I tell you, there will be rejoicing among the angels of God over one sinner who repents." (Luke 15:1–10)

I remember meeting Frank many years ago as he walked down the street past the church where I worked. Many teens had told me Frank was a problem teen. When I said, "Hi," he said, "You don't want to know me."

That saddened me. Frank, a freshman, had accepted his reputation and saw himself as a problem.

But God never sees anyone as a problem. Jesus makes that clear in this week's Gospel. In fact, Jesus shows how God goes above and beyond to love people who struggle with faith.

That's hard for humans. We can be quick to label people as problems. Or, we look at our own failures and give up on ourselves, just like Frank did. So if you've ever felt that way, you're not alone.

This Gospel offers two challenges. First, don't write yourself off. Sin doesn't anger God; it moves God's compassion. So turn toward God. Pray. Go to confession. Seek guidance from an adult you trust. Let God's compassion embrace you and your faults. That compassion will help you start over.

Second, don't write anyone else off. Each person has a talent the world needs. Ask God to help you see the potential in people who seem to struggle with sin or failure. You can be God's encouragement to them.

God helped me reach out to Frank when he saw himself as a problem. He eventually helped start a parish retreat program, and his life made a huge difference to other teens.

That's why God never gives up!

Take :10 Reflect

If a word or phrase from the Gospel grabs your heart, sit quietly for several minutes, repeating it to yourself and asking God to show you how it applies to your life. Or, reflect and possibly journal on the following questions:

• Have you ever felt like giving up on yourself? Why?

What's Wealth Really Worth?

Take :05 Examine

How did I live out last week's Gospel message? What was tough? What was rewarding?

Take :05 Read

Jesus said to his disciples, "A rich man had a steward who was reported to him for squandering his property. He summoned him and said, 'What is this I hear about you? Prepare a full account of your stewardship, because you can no longer be my steward.' The steward said to himself, 'What shall I do, now that my master is taking the position of steward away from me? I am not strong enough to dig and I am ashamed to beg. I know what I shall do so that, when I am removed from the stewardship, they may welcome me into their homes.' He called in his master's debtors one by one. To the first he said, 'How much do you owe my master?' He replied, 'One hundred measures of olive oil.' He said to him, 'Here is your promissory note. Sit down and quickly write one for fifty.' Then to another the steward said, 'And you, how much do you owe?' He replied, 'One hundred kors of wheat.' The steward said to him, 'Here is your promissory note; write one for eighty.' And the master commended that dishonest steward for acting prudently.

. . . If, therefore, you are not trustworthy with dishonest wealth, who will trust you with true wealth? If you are not trustworthy with what belongs to another, who will give you what is yours? No servant can serve two masters. He will either hate one and love the other, or be devoted to one and despise the other. You cannot serve both God and mammon." (Luke 16:1–8a, 11–13)

Oscar Schindler was a rich man who learned the real value of wealth.

Schindler was a successful German factory owner during World War II. He made his wealth mostly by joining the Nazi party and exploiting Jewish workers.

But Schindler changed during the war. He became sickened by his complicity in Germany's treatment of Jews. Eventually, he spent his fortune and went broke buying safety for about twelve hundred Jews who would have died in death camps. His story connects well with this week's Gospel and its message about wealth.

First, our wealth should serve our relationships, not vice versa. Jesus isn't advising us to act like the steward and use other people's money dishonestly. Rather, he's pointing out that we'll find more security and meaning in life if we use our wealth generously for others. We'll have less stuff than others, but our lives will be rich in relationships.

Second, we can't claim the title Christian unless we consciously choose God as our Master. And that means we need to ask ourselves this basic question: I serve God, so how would God have me use my wealth, money, talent, and time?

That's a tough question. But if you ask it daily in prayer, you'll start to see the world and respond to it like Oscar Schindler did.

Take :10 Reflect

If a word or phrase from the Gospel grabs your heart, sit quietly for several minutes, repeating it to yourself and asking God to show you how it applies to your life. Or, reflect and possibly journal on the following question:

- What might change in your life if you looked at your talent, time, and money like Oscar Schindler did?

Who's Outside Your Door?

Take :05 Examine

How did I live out last week's Gospel message? What was tough? What was rewarding?

Take :05 Read

Jesus said to the Pharisees: "There was a rich man who dressed in purple garments and fine linen and dined sumptuously each day. And lying at his door was a poor man named Lazarus, covered with sores, who would gladly have eaten his fill of the scraps that fell from the rich man's table. Dogs even used to come and lick his sores. When the poor man died, he was carried away by angels to the bosom of Abraham. The rich man also died and was buried, and from the netherworld, where he was in torment, he raised his eyes and saw Abraham far off and Lazarus at his side. And he cried out, 'Father Abraham, have pity on me. Send Lazarus to dip the tip of his finger in water and cool my tongue, for I am suffering torment in these flames.' Abraham replied, 'My child, remember that you received what was good during your lifetime while Lazarus likewise received what was bad; but now he is comforted here, whereas you are tormented.' . . . He said, 'Then I beg you, father, send him to my father's house, for I have five brothers, so that he may warn them, lest they too come to this place of torment.' But Abraham replied, 'They have Moses and the prophets. Let them listen to them.' He said, 'Oh no, father Abraham, but if someone from the dead goes to them, they will repent.' Then Abraham said, 'If they will not listen to Moses and the prophets, neither will they be persuaded if someone should rise from the dead.'" (Luke 16:19–25,27–31)

Have you ever noticed that this rich man never did anything wrong? He just went about his life. For whatever reason, he didn't even notice Lazarus. Maybe he was just busy. Who knows?

And that, Jesus says, is the problem. It's not what the rich man did. It's what he didn't do.

Life gets busy. I know adults that work hard all day and then spend the evening driving their kids to activities. I know teens that go to school all day and then spend each evening on homework, sports, or school activities.

But Lazarus lives today. He is the lonely kid at school. He is the hungry child in Africa. Jesus challenges us to care for him regularly. Make it part of your "busyness," not something you fit in when you find extra time.

Here are some tips. Ask God daily to show you the people others ignore. Read newspapers to learn about the problems that cause suffering in our world. Make service trips and peace rallies part of your monthly schedule.

God has given you the power to change the world for people who suffer like Lazarus. Who's lying outside your door?

Take :10 Reflect

If a word or phrase from the Gospel grabs your heart, sit quietly for several minutes, repeating it to yourself and asking God to show you how it applies to your life. Or, reflect and possibly journal on the following question:

• What's one thing you do to keep your focus on people like Lazarus?

God's in Charge . . . You're Free!

Take :05 Examine

How did I live out last week's Gospel message? What was tough? What was rewarding?

Take :05 Read

The apostles said to the Lord, "Increase our faith." The Lord replied, "If you have faith the size of a mustard seed, you would say to this mulberry tree, 'Be uprooted and planted in the sea,' and it would obey you.

"Who among you would say to your servant who has just come in from plowing or tending sheep in the field, 'Come here immediately and take your place at table'? Would he not rather say to him, 'Prepare something for me to eat. Put on your apron and wait on me while I eat and drink. You may eat and drink when I am finished'? Is he grateful to that servant because he did what was commanded? So should it be with you. When you have done all you have been commanded, say, 'We are unprofitable servants; we have done what we were obliged to do.'"

It's very predictable. Often when I talk with a group of high school students, I ask who would like more freedom from parents. Most hands shoot up.

It's normal for teens to thirst for freedom, just like it's normal for parents to get nervous about granting it. But this week's Gospel is all about freedom—the freedom that comes when you realize God's in charge and you're not.

Our culture is pretty competitive. Who will get the best grades? Who will win the game? Who will look the best? It's easy for life to become nothing but one long final exam where success means everything. And that's when life becomes pretty meaningless. Jesus offers us so much by reminding us that we're God's servants.

But how's that better? After all, who wants to be a servant when they grow up?

It's better because it frees us. God's in charge. We can't solve the world's problems. That's God's job. So don't worry about being a successful Christian. God asks you only to faithfully do what you can, remembering that God's love doesn't depend on your success.

We're free. We're free to take risks for our faith because we don't need to worry about success. A lot of teens have inspired me by that willingness. "What have I got to lose?" they've said as they've signed up for service trips or joined youth groups. And the more you risk things for God, the Master, the more you'll get what the Apostles wanted in this week's Gospel: more faith. Risking for faith is like lifting weights—it builds spiritual muscle.

What a gift God has given us by taking charge. In a world where you might feel responsible for so much, enjoy the freedom that comes from being God's servant.

Take :10 Reflect

If a word or phrase from the Gospel grabs your heart, sit quietly for several minutes, repeating it to yourself and asking God to show you how it applies to your life. Or, reflect and possibly journal on the following question:

- Does your fear of failure ever stop you from taking risks for your faith?

You Fit In with Jesus

Take :05 Examine

How did I live out last week's Gospel message? What was tough? What was rewarding?

Take :05 Read

As Jesus continued his journey to Jerusalem, he traveled through Samaria and Galilee. As he was entering a village, ten lepers met him. They stood at a distance from him and raised their voices, saying, "Jesus, Master! Have pity on us!" And when he saw them, he said, "Go show yourselves to the priests." As they were going they were cleansed. And one of them, realizing he had been healed, returned, glorifying God in a loud voice; and he fell at the feet of Jesus and thanked him. He was a Samaritan. Jesus said in reply, "Ten were cleansed, were they not? Where are the other nine? Has none but this foreigner returned to give thanks to God?" Then he said to him, "Stand up and go; your faith has saved you."

I knew a young man who started high school sure he wouldn't fit in. He remembered how kids made fun of him in junior high. He remembered they always chose him last for teams. He felt so out of place there that he doubted he'd fit in anywhere.

I wish he was rare. But there are many teens that feel like outcasts. They find it hard to fit in with friends because of weight, acne, insecurity, the wrong clothes. . . . The list goes on. You might feel that way now.

That's why this week's Gospel is so important. The Samaritan leper was a double outcast. First, he was a leper. Leprosy in the Gospel isn't the disease that causes limbs to decay. It caused flaky or scaly skin. The Jewish religious laws told Jewish people to avoid contact with people who had it. The Samaritan was also outcast because of his ethnic background. Many Jews rejected Samaritans because they descended from Jews who married non-Jews.

Notice how Jesus reacted to those outcasts. He stopped, noticed their pain, and healed them. That means they could now fit in. People would welcome them. Care about them.

Also notice that the Samaritan was the only one who returned to thank Jesus. Jesus took note that only this "foreigner" seemed grateful.

The point for us?

First, if you feel like you don't fit in anywhere, call out to Jesus for help like the lepers in the Gospel. Call out through prayer. Call out by talking to an adult who you trust. Call out by getting involved in serving other people who suffer. You'll find that he'll answer your prayers. You'll find a place to fit in and friends who care.

Second, Jesus points out that the Samaritan, the double outcast, shows more faith than anyone. That means we all need to respect and learn from the people we think don't fit in.

Take :10 Reflect

If a word or phrase from the Gospel grabs your heart, sit quietly for several minutes, repeating it to yourself and asking God to show you how it applies to your life. Or, reflect and possibly journal on the following question:

- Have you ever felt like an outcast or reached out to someone who felt that way?

Prayer and Hangin' Out

Take :05 Examine

How did I live out last week's Gospel message? What was
tough? What was rewarding?

Take :05 Read

*Jesus told his disciples a parable about the necessity for them to
pray always without becoming weary. He said, "There was a
judge in a certain town who neither feared God nor respected
any human being. And a widow in that town used to come to
him and say, 'Render a just decision for me against my adver-
sary.' For a long time the judge was unwilling, but eventually he
thought, 'While it is true that I neither fear God nor respect any
human being, because this widow keeps bothering me I shall
deliver a just decision for her lest she finally come and strike
me.'" The Lord said, "Pay attention to what the dishonest judge
says. Will not God then secure the rights of his chosen ones who
call out to him day and night? Will he be slow to answer them? I
tell you, he will see to it that justice is done for them speedily. But
when the Son of Man comes, will he find faith on earth?"*

Pray always?

Some scholars translate this as praying without ceasing.
Sounds pretty impossible. But maybe it depends on how
you look at it.

Here's how I pictured prayer when I was young. Kneeling
at church. Reciting memorized prayers. Lying in bed, asking
for help on a test or with a friend. Prayer took time set
aside. So you could never pray always, unless you never ate,
studied, or worked.

Over the years I've come to see God as my friend, a constant companion, always there to support and guide me. So my understanding of prayer has changed. I still think it's important to set aside special time for prayer, but I've learned that I don't need to wait for those times. God's hangin' out with me all day long.

And that's pretty critical for me. Because several times each day I need divine help. It happens like this. Here's that person who irritates me. God, give me patience. Here's someone asking for help. God, what do I do? I feel like an idiot. God, help me believe in myself. What a beautiful day. God, help me be grateful.

God surrounds us each moment of our lives. Jesus, in this week's Gospel, told his disciples to recognize that and rejoice. We all want close friends willing to hang out with us. Some of us have them. Some don't. But we all have a best friend in God, who is always trying to shape us, help us, respond to us.

Here's a challenge: Pray always, or without ceasing, this week. Make an effort to remember that God walks with you at all times, down every school hallway, across every practice field, through every mall, and across every street. Talk and listen to God throughout the day. In other words, just hang out together.

Take :10 Reflect

If a word or phrase from the Gospel grabs your heart, sit quietly for several minutes, repeating it to yourself and asking God to show you how it applies to your life. Or, reflect and possibly journal on the following question:

• What insights about prayer does this reflection offer you?

Exalted Sinners?

Take :05 Examine

How did I live out last week's Gospel message? What was tough? What was rewarding?

Take :05 Read

Jesus addressed this parable to those who were convinced of their own righteousness and despised everyone else. "Two people went up to the temple area to pray; one was a Pharisee and the other was a tax collector. The Pharisee took up his position and spoke this prayer to himself, 'O God, I thank you that I am not like the rest of humanity—greedy, dishonest, adulterous—or even like this tax collector. I fast twice a week, and I pay tithes on my whole income.' But the tax collector stood off at a distance and would not even raise his eyes to heaven but beat his breast and prayed, 'O God, be merciful to me a sinner.' I tell you, the latter went home justified, not the former; for whoever exalts himself will be humbled, and the one who humbles himself will be exalted."

I wish it wasn't true, but when it comes to sin, I know it well. In fact, I'm an expert.

I remember many times in my life when I've had trouble looking myself in the mirror. "You are a jerk," I've thought to myself. "You call yourself a Christian? If people only knew the *real* you."

But over the years I've learned to thank God that Jesus does know the *real* me, with all my sins and hang-ups. I've learned to face them honestly. Why? Jesus can't heal what I hide.

We all have done things we're ashamed of. We all have sinful habits we'd like to break. And this week's Gospel reminds us that the only real remedy is gut-wrenching honesty with God, who is mercy, compassion, and healing.

Here's the truth. Secrets kill. The more we keep sinful mistakes and habits secret, the more we give them power over our lives. They control us until we are humble enough to "beat our breast" (an ancient act that showed sorrow) and say, "O God, be merciful to me a sinner." Use the sacrament of Penance and Reconciliation. It is a perfect way to air our sins and let someone remind us about God's love while giving us advice on how to change. See a spiritual director, an older Christian you respect with whom you meet regularly to discuss ways of growing closer to God.

Take it from a sinner. God has exalted me when I've admitted how I've sunk into sin. Christ has provided me with priests and spiritual directors who've helped me feel better about myself and grow closer to God by looking with compassion at my sins and flaws. It's difficult and humbling, but God has always picked me up and never let me down.

Take :10 Reflect

If a word or phrase from the Gospel grabs your heart, sit quietly for several minutes, repeating it to yourself and asking God to show you how it applies to your life. Or, reflect and possibly journal on the following question:

- From what secret sins and shame do you need freedom?

A Good Role Model

How did I live out last week's Gospel message? What was tough? What was rewarding?

At that time, Jesus came to Jericho and intended to pass through the town. Now a man there named Zacchaeus, who was a chief tax collector and also a wealthy man, was seeking to see who Jesus was; but he could not see him because of the crowd, for he was short in stature. So he ran ahead and climbed a sycamore tree in order to see Jesus, who was about to pass that way. When he reached the place, Jesus looked up and said, "Zacchaeus, come down quickly, for today I must stay at your house." And he came down quickly and received him with joy. When they all saw this, they began to grumble, saying, "He has gone to stay at the house of a sinner." But Zacchaeus stood there and said to the Lord, "Behold, half of my possessions, Lord, I shall give to the poor, and if I have extorted anything from anyone I shall repay it four times over." And Jesus said to him, "Today salvation has come to this house because this man too is a descendant of Abraham. For the Son of Man has come to seek and to save what was lost."

That guy Zacchaeus is one of my heroes. He was a little guy. Maybe he was pushed around much of his life by bigger people. The "in crowd" looked down upon him. He collected taxes for the Romans, so there couldn't have been anything good about him.

But Zacchaeus had guts. He couldn't see Jesus, so he climbed a tree. His job as a tax collector also gave him the power to abuse people, but he told Jesus he would repay people "four times over" if he had treated them unjustly. He also had great wealth but pledged to share it with the poor.

In this week's Gospel, Jesus teaches by making Zacchaeus a role model. Religious people were shocked that Jesus would dine with Zacchaeus. But Jesus, unlike them, saw the man's heart and scolded onlookers for judging Zacchaeus.

Zacchaeus can be our role model too. And I bet if you look around, you'll see Christians just like him. I have friends who constantly go out of their way to see Jesus' spirit in people I write off. They remind me of Zacchaeus. I have friends who will quickly admit their wrongs and make things right. They remind me of Zacchaeus. I have friends who have great wealth but focus more on sharing it with the poor than on protecting it for themselves. They remind me of Zacchaeus. I have friends who have been pushed around and belittled. They've never been part of the "in crowd." But they don't act bitter. They focus on living a good life. They remind me of Zacchaeus.

I bet if you look around your school, parish, or family, you'll see Zacchaeus. You might catch a glimpse of him if you look in your mirror. I bet people see some of Zacchaeus in you too. Don't sell yourself short.

Take :10 Reflect

If a word or phrase from the Gospel grabs your heart, sit quietly for several minutes, repeating it to yourself and asking God to show you how it applies to your life. Or, reflect and possibly journal on the following question:

• Whom do you know that reminds you of Zacchaeus?

Don't Close Your Mind to God

Take :05 Examine

How did I live out last week's Gospel message? What was
tough? What was rewarding?

Take :05 Read

*Some Sadducees, those who deny that there is a resurrection,
came forward. . . . Jesus said to them, "The children of this age
marry and remarry; but those who are deemed worthy to attain
to the coming age and to the resurrection of the dead neither
marry nor are given in marriage. They can no longer die, for they
are like angels; and they are the children of God because they
are the ones who will rise. That the dead will rise even Moses
made known in the passage about the bush, when he called out
'Lord,' the God of Abraham, the God of Isaac, and the God of
Jacob; and he is not God of the dead, but of the living, for to him
all are alive." (Luke 20:27,34–38)*

I wrote a regular newspaper column in college. I usually
knew *for sure* I was right about an issue and attacked
opposing arguments by making fun of them. My mind was
closed, just like the Sadducees' in this week's Gospel.

The Sadducees were members of a religious group
whose beliefs differed from Jesus' teachings. For example,
they didn't believe in the Resurrection or in angels. But in
this week's Gospel, they didn't listen to him and rethink
their positions; instead, they made an argument that
mocked his beliefs.

That's too common in our society. People don't listen to
one another; instead, they attack or belittle one another. It's

an easy style to adopt. You don't have to think if you can shout down or mock your opponent.

But that's how you miss God's wisdom. This week's Gospel reminds us that sometimes God challenges our positions on things like religion, school, and family. That challenge will likely come through friends, pastors, teachers, and family members. The Spirit calls us to keep our minds open, especially to people with whom we disagree.

Here are some tips:

- When you disagree with someone, avoid the temptation to close your mind or respond with sarcasm or personal attacks. Think. Ask God to help you consider opposing opinions closely.

- Don't let pride get in the way. God calls us to full life, but we miss out—like the Sadducees did—when we're not open to the spiritual and intellectual changes that life brings.

Take :10 Reflect

If a word or phrase from the Gospel grabs your heart, sit quietly for several minutes, repeating it to yourself and asking God to show you how it applies to your life. Or, reflect and possibly journal on the following question:

- What makes it tough for you to keep your mind open when you disagree with someone?

It's About Perseverance, Not Perfection

Take :05 Examine

How did I live out last week's Gospel message? What was
tough? What was rewarding?

Take :05 Read

*While some people were speaking about how the temple was
adorned with costly stones and votive offerings, Jesus said, "All
that you see here—the days will come when there will not be
left a stone upon another stone that will not be thrown down."*

*Then they asked him, "Teacher, when will this happen? And
what sign will there be when all these things are about to
happen?" He answered, "See that you not be deceived, for many
will come in my name, saying, 'I am he,' and 'The time has come.'
Do not follow them! When you hear of wars and insurrections,
do not be terrified; for such things must happen first, but it will
not immediately be the end. . . .*

*"Before all this happens, however, they will seize and perse-
cute you, they will hand you over to the synagogues and to
prisons, and they will have you led before kings and governors
because of my name. It will lead to your giving testimony. Remember, you are not to prepare your defense beforehand, for I
myself shall give you a wisdom in speaking that all your adver-
saries will be powerless to resist or refute. You will even be handed over by parents, brothers, relatives, and friends, and they will
put some of you to death. You will be hated by all because of my
name, but not a hair on your head will be destroyed. By your
perseverance you will secure your lives." (Luke 21:5–9, 12–19)*

Progress, not perfection. That phrase is critical to recovering alcoholics. Many cling to it because they are tempted to give up on sobriety when they make a mistake and drink. Don't give up, they remind one another. Perfection is impossible. But God can help you progress, one step at a time, toward a healthy life.

Christians can learn a lot from recovering alcoholics.

We'll never be perfect disciples. We're human and face tough temptations. Wear these clothes—you'll fit in. Drink this—you'll have friends. Cheat—you need the grade. Laugh at them—don't be a loser.

We're going to trip up.

The early Christians faced tough choices too. Luke included this Gospel passage to warn his community about people who claimed Jesus had returned and "the end was near." This Gospel story also reminds folks that Christ stands with us through temptation, persecution, and even failure.

It's tough out there. But remember, Jesus says we secure our lives through perseverance as Christians. That means we need to keep trying. Over time we'll see progress in our Christian living, and we'll worry less about perfection.

Take :10 Reflect

If a word or phrase from the Gospel grabs your heart, sit quietly for several minutes, repeating it to yourself and asking God to show you how it applies to your life. Or, reflect and possibly journal on the following question:

- What tempts teens to give up on trying to live the Christian life?

Come, Follow This "Failed" King

Take :05 Examine

How did I live out last week's Gospel message? What was tough? What was rewarding?

Take :05 Read

The rulers sneered at Jesus and said, "He saved others, let him save himself if he is the chosen one, the Christ of God." Even the soldiers jeered at him. As they approached to offer him wine they called out, "If you are King of the Jews, save yourself." Above him there was an inscription that read, "This is the King of the Jews."

Now one of the criminals hanging there reviled Jesus, saying, "Are you not the Christ? Save yourself and us." The other, however, rebuking him, said in reply, "Have you no fear of God, for you are subject to the same condemnation? And indeed, we have been condemned justly, for the sentence we received corresponds to our crimes, but this man has done nothing criminal." Then he said, "Jesus, remember me when you come into your kingdom." He replied to him, "Amen, I say to you, today you will be with me in Paradise."

Our king was a failure. He pushed for a world that welcomed the weak, the powerless, the outsider. So the powerful killed him. He gathered close followers who believed in him and his message. But most of them, including his best friend, abandoned him. He preached that nonviolence could defeat violence. And he suffered the most violent death imaginable.

Our king was a failure. What does that mean for us?

Let's start by remembering our failures. Have your hopes ever been crushed? Have you ever been betrayed, or ever suffered, for doing the right thing? Do you ever feel like a total screwup?

If so, then our King understands you. He's been there, done that. You'll never be alone in your pain. I'll pledge loyalty to a king like that. Will you? Are you looking for a kingdom of forgiveness and hope, peace and justice; a kingdom where you need not be a success; a kingdom where you can always start over?

If so, then call out to Jesus today. Ask for help to make the Kingdom of God real in your life. Forgive when others say get even. Reach out when others pull back. Dream about a better world. Let those dreams inspire you to a life of service even while others surrender to selfishness. The Kingdom is here now. You only need to enter.

And our "failed" King will strengthen you when some mock and attack you. It can get tough building his Kingdom. But it's worth the struggle. And never forget. Even though our King "failed" on Friday, he rose on Sunday.

Take :10 Reflect

If a word or phrase from the Gospel grabs your heart, sit quietly for several minutes, repeating it to yourself and asking God to show you how it applies to your life. Or, reflect and possibly journal on the following question:

- How can teens find comfort in this passage or in following a "failed" King?